Before Logic

RICHARD MASON

State University of New York Press

The extract from "Engführung" by Paul Celan on page 111 is from
Sprachgitter, S. Fischer Verlag, Frankfurt am Main, 1959.

Published by
State University of New York Press, Albany

© 2000 State University of New York

For information, address State University of New York Press,
State University Plaza, Albany, NY 12246

Production, Laurie Searl
Marketing, Michael Campochiaro

Library of Congress Cataloging-in-Publication Data

Mason Richard.
    Before logic / Richard Mason.
        p.   cm. — (SUNY series in philosophy)
    Includes bibliographical references and index.
    ISBN 0-7914-4531-3 (hc : alk. paper) — ISBN 0-7914-4532-1 (pbk. : alk. paper)
        1. Logic. I. Title. II. Series.

BC50.M36 2000
160—dc21
                                                                    99-059365

10 9 8 7 6 5 4 3 2 1

to Margie

CONTENTS

INTRODUCTION

What could come before logic? Some significant choices have to be made before logic—or a logic—can be developed. The outcomes of these choices make real differences to the directions in which logic is developed. Some problems normally thought to be within logic—logical problems—have their origins in the points and directions from which logic has developed. So logic cannot be a prior element in philosophy. Too much comes before it. More loosely, what is accepted as logical may not be taken for granted.

In the broadest outline these views should be neither controversial nor unfamiliar. The thinking in Aristotle's *Categories* and *de Interpretatione* set some of the scene for the logic of the *Analytics*. Something parallel to the general case was argued (in a very different way) in Heidegger's *Metaphysical Foundations of Logic*. The general argument was also implicit in Wittgenstein's movement away from his early view that "logic must take care of itself."[1] The idea that *some* important philosophy has to come before logic is too vague and too anodyne to be debated seriously. The nature and relevance of that philosophy are less obvious. The aim of this book is to offer illustrative studies where choices can be seen, and where their effects are important; also, to show how some specific problems in philosophical logic arise in different ways or with differing force, depending on the directions from which they are approached. So the strength of the general case will depend on the specific substance that can be given to it. This should be constructive as well as critical.

Chapter 1, What can be, considers logical possibility and looks at assumptions behind its use in philosophical thought-experiments. Logical possibility has a curious history. Its support was strangely nonempirical for an archetypal tool in empiricist thinking. The links between historical context and philosophical or logical justification need to be examined. Logical or absolute *im*possibility can be seen as basic to a conception of inference, and hence to much logical thought.

Chapter 2, The truth in what we say, looks at truth as a value and its association with our use of language. Propositional truth—or, more non-committally, the truth of what we say—will be seen to be derivative from, not fundamental to, a wider notion of the true as a value. The indefinability of truth in a language may be seen as a consequence of an insensitivity to a wider understanding. Problems of reference—of opacity and propositional identity—may be created by the direction from which they are approached, from assumptions that a certain kind of truth is possible.

Chapter 3, What must be so, deals with problems in the explanation of necessity. The general challenge presented by necessity—as being in need of explanation at all—will be discussed, rather than specific explanatory or reductive theories (such as conventionalism or constructivism). The need to explain necessity can vary according to the understanding of the necessity which is to be explained. Far more controversially, there is a link (in both directions) between views about the possibility of the explanation of modality and views about the nature of modality. More specifically, necessary truth is a notion which has to create problems of explanation because of the interpretation of modality which it suggests. As in chapter 1, there are consequences for the working of logical thought.

Chapter 4, Talking about things, gives an extended example of how logical problems can be related to starting points in philosophical approach. Problems connected with essentialism may be seen as an outcome of a conflict in approaches. How we talk about things, in a general way, affects the logic we use, which in turn molds how we think about things. The imprecision of these influences is significant.

Chapter 5, Getting around language, investigates the relation between what we say and how things are. The location of logical thinking, in how things are or in what we say about them, is one of the most protean philosophical questions. It has connections with questions raised in the previous chapters: questions on the notion of the limits to what may be said or thought, on the force of logical inference, and on the choices made about the presentation of truth.

The final chapter, "Logic must take care of itself," evaluates the independence and priority of logic, and draws together the preceding arguments. Nietzsche declared that philosophers had erred in "mistaking the last for the first."

> They put that which comes at the end—unfortunately! for it ought not to come at all!—the "highest concepts," that is to say the most general, the emptiest concepts, the last fumes of evaporating reality, at

the beginning, *as* the beginning. It is again only the expression of their way of doing reverence: the higher must not be *allowed* to grow out of the lower, must not be *allowed* to have grown at all . . .[2]

〜

The ordering of the chapters in this book is meant to be neither rigid nor accidental in that they should add up to a case, but not an exhaustive or exclusive one. Usually, logical investigations proceed from meaning and truth to modality, encouraged by the usual exposition (in formal terms) from propositional calculus to modal propositional logic and on to quantified modal logic. Neither that order nor its reverse is implied here. The apparent prominence given to questions about possibility and necessity is not a claim for the priority of modal logics. Instead, it is related to the force or inexorability of logical thinking, which is rooted in assumptions about what cannot be thought and what must be so.

The opening sentence of this introduction—about choices to be made before we start logic—may seem to beg almost every question. It may suggest that there are alternatives in logic—or alternative logics—and that we can make choices between them. It looks foundationalist, in suggesting that logic must have a starting point, or transcendentalist, in suggesting that there are conditions which make logic possible. It suggests that such conditions might be historical rather than logical or philosophical, opening the way for speculation on the historical conditions of logical thought. The remainder of this introduction is intended to clarify the approach to be followed, making explicit the assumptions in the background. Methodology without substance may be empty, but some preliminary ground clearing is unavoidable:

1. Quite apart from the epistemological implications in the idea that logic (or thought) has (or should have) foundations, to look for any set of foundational propositions or philosophical axioms would be directly contrary to the argument here. Rather, the case will be that thought about logic comes from needs and assumptions which are indistinct and sometimes overlapping or even conflicting. So this is not intended as a study of the *foundations* of logic or of logical thought; rather, it can be seen as a study of the tools that could have dug the foundations, if there were any.

2. A helpful first step may be to argue transcendentally: that in fact we think in a certain way—we make certain judgments—and that we could not think in that way unless we somehow presupposed certain beliefs. With

that type of argument, the *we* and the *somehow* conceal virtually everything of real interest. There is not only a confusion between psychological and allegedly logical inquiry (a confusion which some modern commentators claim to have disentangled on behalf of Kant[3]), but also a disregard for historical perspective: who are *we* who are said to think in a particular way? How are we said to have come to think in that way? At what points were alternatives excluded? What difference did that make? The belief that rationality—or some minimal form of logic—is a transcendental condition either for thinking or for the use of language is surprisingly pervasive. Even for philosophers who repudiate the psychologistic naiveté of logic as The Laws of Thought, there can be a slippery slope between logic, thinking in logic, logical thought, logical thinking, logically ordered thinking, rational thinking, and rationality. Chapters 5 and 6 touch on this theme.

3. This book could not be described usefully as a study in the philosophy of logic, and still less in metalogic. Almost nothing will be said about formal systems, and nothing at all will be assumed about the value of any particular formal systems. The idea of a philosophy of logic seems to imply that logic, or a logic, exists, and that we can devote some philosophical thought to it as an object.[4] The notion of metalogic may be meant to imply a more tidily ordered activity or study, itself perhaps wholly or partly formal. Here, on the contrary, in discussing choices made before logic, no position is assumed on the nature of logic beyond loose assumptions that it deals with inconsistency and inference. It is assumed, negatively, that logic is not *only* a formalized system (or more than one system) where the philosophical problem is not *only* one of interpretation or modelling. If that were so, the only perceptible step before logic would be the acquisition of a pencil and paper with which to record it. As Hilbert himself wrote, ". . . the symbolism must come later and in response to a need, from which it follows, of course, that whoever wants to create or develop a symbolism must first study those needs."[5]

4. At the opposite extreme, nothing will be said about the paradoxical-sounding topic of the sociology of logic. Following Lévy-Bruhl, work in that area, though not under that title, has concentrated on the study of alleged transitions to logically ordered thought from mythological, nonrational or prerational thought. In principle, there need be no objection to such an enterprise.[6] Maybe it is true, for example, that thinking in accordance with the principle of the excluded middle has arisen in certain social conditions (where there has been some attachment to monotheism, for

example), and that explicit discovery or enunciation of the principle has followed on. Brouwer wrote that "The long belief in the universal validity of the principle of the excluded third in mathematics is considered by intuitionism as a phenomenon of history of civilization of the same kind as the old-time belief in the rationality of π or in the rotation of the firmament on an axis passing through the earth,"[7] but his serious attention was directed to the logical consequences of that view, rather than its historical vindication. On the other hand, it must be truer than most logicians would wish to recognize that notions such as necessity *have* arisen in particular contexts, and their subsequent development has taken place and may well have been influenced by factors which are wholly outside any conception of logic.[8]

Turning in a more positive direction, this book argues that there is an undeniable and essentially historical dimension to logic. When we talk about concepts of inference or necessity we tend to mean *our* concepts, and when we talk about our concepts we tend to mean our concepts *now*, which may not be the same as others' concepts at other times. A central strand in the argument will be that some—apparently purely logical— notions acquire their senses within specific frameworks, and that some of the apparently purely logical problems surrounding them tend to arise when those frameworks are removed or denied. Both logical possibility and necessary truth will be approached in this way. The lines to be followed will not be those of Frege, most extremely, who wrote: "A logical concept does not develop and it does not have a history, at least not in the currently fashionable sense . . . I see no great need for being able to talk about the history of the development of a concept, and I find that there is good reason to avoid this phrase. . . ."[9] So before logic can certainly be taken, in part, in a temporal, historical sense. There have been real points of historical choice, at or after which things could have been different. In the final chapter it will be argued that it is the nonreversible change which matters in this notion of historical choice, not the seemingly ontological question of whether the same or different concepts exist at different times. But there are good reasons not to pursue a wholly historical argument. The actual history of logic is both thin and highly discontinuous.[10] The orthodox, one-sentence caricature-history of logic is not too incorrect: the subject did indeed come into existence with Aristotle; its philosophical background was explored and charted by Leibniz; and it was transfigured almost into its modern form by Frege before its great explosion of activity in the twentieth century.

Some of the topics in this book could as well be approached textually, in detailed studies of the writings of Aristotle, Leibniz, or Frege. That approach has not been followed here, partly because of the potential narrowing or loss of focus, partly because of wariness about entanglement in straightforwardly textual debate, and partly because such a directly historical perspective would be misleading. (Heidegger's *Metaphysical Foundations of Logic*, concentrating on Leibniz, ran into all these hazards.) It may be true, for instance, that Aristotle chose to see essence in terms of essential properties rather than in terms of essential parts or ingredients (this will be discussed in chapter 4). Such a choice may have had consequences for the development of logic and the natural sciences. Here we may see a specific point of choice, identifiable in specific philosophical texts. It is possible to see essence in terms of essential properties or essential ingredients (or both, or in some other way); essence has, as a matter of fact, been seen largely in one way rather than another. There does seem to have been an historical point of choice between ways of seeing it, and this point may be identifiable, but it is not important if it is not.

The notion of a 'starting point' will occur several times in the book. It should not be understood in a foundational or axiomatic way, in the sense of some tenet or set of tenets on which others depend logically. Nor should it be seen in a specifically historical sense, as a datable point in the chronological development of logic. Rather, it can be characterized as a significant point of choice of perspective or direction, where significance is measured in terms of extensive effects. One example has just come up: the starting point from which different forms of description can diverge—in one direction towards predicative accounts, in another towards constitutive accounts. A more central example is given in chapter 3, where it will be argued that a perspective based on an assumption that necessity is to be seen as necessary truth may have radical effects within logic. Such starting points may be historically datable. The Kneales rightly described 1879, the year of publication of Frege's *Begriffsschrift*, as the most important date in the history of logic.[11] There can be a strong empirical element, in that the reasons behind a divergence of interests may not have much to do with logical or philosophical considerations. Still, the notion of a starting point is intrinsically nonformal and nonsystematic. We may judge things through a number of perspectives which may have developed from different starting points for differing, and not necessarily consistent or independent, reasons. This should not be assumed to be undesirable; on the contrary, philosophical trouble may originate from the kind of reductionism which seeks to straitjacket perspectives into a single norm.

The approach in this book can be seen as widely historical. What follows could also be called a kind of *deconstruction*, if that term had not been taken over for totally different purposes, to the extent that its use here would be seriously misleading. Using a less loaded word, we can *dismantle* a notion such as logical possibility to see how and where it originated, and in what context it was supposed to be used. This dismantling may be historical, in the sense of tracing roots. It may be quasi-logical, in showing how differing perspectives can be disentangled from each other. It may be both at once, as illustrated in chapter 4, where part of the argument will be that different perspectives—or attention to different aspects of things—may be maintained without error, and without relativism, at the same time. Problems may arise when we try to reduce one perspective—or, at any rate, reduce it too crudely—to another, or where we try to use the language of one perspective to speak too simply about things which another style of language may have been developed (or may have evolved) to describe.

Dismantling or deconstructing, like *analysis*, is a metaphor. As with analysis, it would be sensible not to insist on too literal an understanding. Just two points can be noted about the approach to be followed, perhaps in contrast with a more orthodox analytical method, if any such thing still survives.

First, in trying to take apart some central elements in our thinking, we cannot avoid looking at the context in which they have evolved or developed. This, as we have seen, brings in an historical dimension. That is not optional.

Second, no claim is made about any particular attitude to what is studied, though this is not an attempt to attain some utopia of neutrality. At one extreme there is the view that we "may in no way interfere with the actual use of language"; we may only describe, "leave everything as it is." Any opposition between such a descriptive approach and some kind of stipulative revision must be a false one.[12] A work about logic may or may not be a work of logic. A work of logic may or may not be about logic. In seeking to take apart some central elements in logic, we cannot guarantee that the pieces will look the same to us if we want to put them together again. Neither legitimation nor disendorsement can be achieved by dismantling, or by history, or by analysis alone. To understand the nature, including the origins, of our logical apparatus may give us confidence in its use or may persuade us to modify or give up its use, no presupposition need be made.

This may be a point where the models expressing our thought have some influence. Mechanical imagery—apparatus, machinery, systems—suggests that logic, like a clock, can be taken apart and reassembled without

damage. Maybe it can, but the use of this sort of language is clearly not accidental. We can ponder the implications of a shift from mechanical to biological imagery (by no means the same as a shift from objective to subjective or from realist to constructivist). Not all dissections and amputations
leave a patient in good health, or even alive. The idea that mechanical
imagery is more neutral when we talk about logic is itself far from neutral.

～

   Lastly, in introduction, it may seem that the pass has already been sold
on the nature of logic. Choices suggest alternatives. The development of
logical concepts suggests that logic may change. The impression may be one
of covert conceptualism: an implication that logic is to be studied in our
logical concepts, through which we judge (or have to judge) reality, or in
our logical language, with which we speak about it. Starting points or perspectives seem to suggest a genetic relativism in which logical concepts may
be legitimized within their context of use. Such positions would leave room
for traditional debates about the discovery or creation of our logical concepts and would allow for discussion of any relation between "our concepts" and "reality" (or "the given") but would shut the door on more fundamental issues. This will be discussed in chapters 5 and 6.
   In fact, almost everything is given away in starting to think about logical concepts in contrast with—over against—reality. Hilbert asked: "Can
thought about things be so much different from things? Can thinking
processes be so unlike the actual processes of things? In short, can thought
be so far removed from reality?"[13] His questions represent a crucial starting
point in themselves, not just in thought about logic, or within logic, but
before logic.

CHAPTER 1

What can be

In a letter of May 1644 Descartes wrote:

> I turn to the difficulty of conceiving how God would have been act-
> ing freely and indifferently if he had made it false that the three angles
> of a triangle were equal to two right angles, or in general that contra-
> dictories could not be true together. It is easy to dispel this difficulty
> by considering that the power of God cannot have any limits, and that
> our mind is finite and so created as to be able to conceive as possible
> the things which God has wished to be in fact possible, but not to be
> able to conceive as possible things which God could have made pos-
> sible, but which he has nevertheless wished to make impossible. The
> first consideration shows us that God cannot have been determined to
> make it true that contradictories cannot be true together [les contra-
> dictoires ne peuvent être ensemble], and therefore that he could have
> done the opposite. The second consideration assures us that even if this
> be true, we should not try to comprehend it, since our nature is inca-
> pable of doing so.[1]

A few years later, Pascal—who did not like Descartes at all—commented:

> It is a sickness natural to man to believe that he possesses truth directly;
> and from that comes the fact that he is always ready to deny every-
> thing that is incomprehensible to him.[2]

For both Descartes and Pascal the context was theological. Pascal's view,
one might think, was more deeply so. The human mind, as part of fallen

nature, cannot be expected to have special access to truth. More, or worse, "Contradiction is a bad mark of truth: several things that are certain are contradicted; several false things pass without contradiction. Contradiction is not a mark of falsity, nor is noncontradiction a mark of truth": the human intellectual apparatus, wounded by original sin, cannot be trusted to detect either truth or falsity.[3] In any case, the most important facts about the world—that God became man, for example—contain irremovable paradoxes. So what we can conceive or imagine will not get us far, for theological reasons.

In reality, though, Descartes's position was no less grounded in theological assumptions. "Our nature" is incapable of comprehending that contradictories might be true together, because our mind is so created by God as "not to be able to conceive as possible things which God could have made possible, but which he has nevertheless wished to make impossible." We can pass over the question of God's freedom to create impossibilities, later to be so trying for Leibniz, and focus on the divine legitimation for our power of comprehension. This was not dispensable for Descartes. Switching from French to Latin in midsentence, perhaps to underline the solidity of the principle he was citing, he wrote to Mersenne in 1640: "It seems very clear to me that possible existence is contained in everything which we clearly understand, because from the fact that we clearly understand something it follows that it can be created by God."[4] To be conceivable (in Descartes's sense) was to be possible (in Descartes's sense). That contains two theological assumptions: God has made us so that our power of conception works successfully in that way, and possibility-in-principle has to be possibility-in-principle-for God. This was no esoteric byway in Descartes's thinking. The rule he was using appears at the crux of one of his most famous arguments, in the *Sixth Meditation*: "The fact that I can clearly and distinctly understand one thing apart from another is enough to make me certain that the two things are distinct, since they are capable of being separated, at least by God."[5] This thinking relied in important ways on the capacity of our natural powers of conception. They may not model or match God's, but it is the fact that God has made us as we are which legitimizes them. Cognition may be naturalized, but the natural has to be understood in terms of divine creation.[6] Without the underwriting, the logic would be unsupported. W. D. Hart misses this in his discussion of the related "principle that what can be imagined is possible." "As an epistemological principle," he writes, it seems to be connected by analogy with traditional empiricism. At the core of empiricism lies the doctrine that perception is the basic faculty we exercise in justifying beliefs about what is actually true. The analogy is that as perception justifies (some) belief in actual truth, so imagination justifies (some) belief in possible truth; perception is to the actual as imagination is to the possible.[7]

That reverses history in a significant way. The principle being discussed was not a tool of "traditional empiricism" used presciently by Descartes, with a dispensable theological appendage. It was more an element of prerationalist religious thinking that was to stagger forward into empiricism.

Ripped even more thoroughly from any context, in an historical void, the notion of central interest is sketched here by Graeme Forbes:

> As a rough elucidatory guide, "it is possible that P" in the broadly logical sense means that there are ways things might have gone, no matter how improbable they may be, as a result of which it would have come about that P. So in this sense it *is* true, for the typical reader, that it is possible that he is a millionaire today, just as Jones would have been if he had taken his broker's advice.[8]

How far that sort of possibility has any value, outside the contexts or environments which supported it, is the point to be discussed in this chapter. But what those environments were, and when they had their heydays, is a large part of the question. One might think that Hume captured one defining moment—

> no inference from cause to effect amounts to a demonstration. Of which there is this evident proof. The mind can always *conceive* any effect to follow from any cause, and indeed any event to follow upon another: whatever we *conceive* is possible, at least in a metaphysical sense: but wherever a demonstration takes place, the contrary is impossible, and implies a contradiction. There is no demonstration, therefore, for any conjunction of cause and effect. And this is a principle, which is generally allowed by philosophers.[9]

—or that Wittgenstein defined a certain end point or reductio ad absurdum in the *Tractatus*: "A picture contains the possibility of the situation that it represents. . . . What can be described can also happen. . . . The only impossibility that exists is *logical* impossibility."[10]—and the main force of this chapter should be applicable to these two examples. Uncontroversially, some notion of logical possibility was essential to the type of philosophical thought-experiment used by Hume. "Whatever we *conceive* is possible, at least in a metaphysical sense" is a cardinal assumption in his argument (though his appeal to a metaphysical sense might set off some alarms, given his professed attitude to many metaphysical matters). The *Tractatus* took that position to its extreme. To be picturable was to be possible. "What can be described can also happen . . ." sounds like the apotheosis of the philosophical thought-experiment.[11]

But the real interest must be in the connection with logic itself. The initial passage quoted from Descartes circles uneasily around the real issue. That *les contradictoires ne peuvent être ensemble,* Descartes well understood, was fundamental. The kind of impossibility that excluded inconsistency must have been prior to logic. Later writers probed the weakness in the use of God's will: the notion that God could have "done the opposite" in some opaque or unintelligible sense. Yet the important point, as Descartes saw, was not what God could do but what we can do. The negative force of inconsistency, and hence the positive force of consistency, related to our nature, which was created by God. If, as David Sanford puts it, logic is "the science of inconsistency,"[12] then that science, for Descartes, was grounded in the capabilities of our nature, and the validity of the science had to be underwritten by God.

⤜

The outline of the case is simple: what we now see as logical possibility is a technical notion. This is undeniable in the harmless sense that some explanation for its use is advisable to avoid confusion. It is also true in a stronger sense, in that we should not assume any uncontroversial interpretation of logical possibility outside some context of explanation. The argument will be that the justification for such a context (or contexts) is questionable. And the argument is an historical one. The initial context for logical possibility was theological. When that became less plausible, the context became psychological: mental representability. When that became implausible, the context came to be logic: purified, absolute representability. But logical possibility provided at least some support for logic. So what support could logic provide for logical possibility? The suggestion is not a vicious circle because, in short, it might make good sense for logic to be fortified by logic. The problem is that logical possibility owed its force to a succession of contexts from a repudiated past. It outlived its history.

THE NEED FOR CONTEXT

It should be seen that *logical possibility* has to be taken as a term of art, mainly in philosophy. That should not be too difficult, as might be recognized by any teacher who has tried to persuade students that it is logically possible to fly unaided to the moon or (using the example just cited) that it is true, for the typical reader, that it is possible that he or she is a millionaire today. Further, logical possibility derives its point from the very fact that it is not like what might be called (without question begging) ordinary possibility. The first step in any explanation of logical possibility should be that it is not like any normal conception of what can happen. Logical possibility has to be less limiting than nonlogical possibility because logical impossibility has to be ultimately restrictive. If something is logically impossible then it is absolutely ruled out, so if it is logically possible, plainly, it may be not absolutely ruled out.

G. E. Moore wrote in his *Commonplace Book* that it was logically possible that he should have been seeing exactly what he was seeing, and yet should have had no eyes.[13] As Moore knew and intended, this was a long way from any normal use of *possible*. People without eyes cannot see. The suggestion that it is logically possible that they might see may need some explanation. For those who may have reservations about this example, a further obstacle lies in wait. One might try to understand possibility in terms of scientific availability. Some story can be told: remarkable scientific developments . . . subsequent evolution in the sense of "seeing" . . . and so on. . . . It might follow that a dogmatic denial of the possibility of seeing without eyes would be unwise. It would not follow that logical possibility was not a wider, more technical notion than practical possibility. One thought in the background could be that a naive sense of *what can happen* could be superseded by a more sophisticated sense of what is possible within the framework of any possible theory. Maybe it could, though that thought is not itself without extreme difficulties in relation to the characterization of a possible theory, but no one could imagine that this was not a radical revision of any everyday understanding. An alternative revisionary view can be given by those who adopt an extremely confident understanding of the intelligibility of what can happen, where *what can happen* is to be understood solely through a network of ("natural") causes, and where logical possibility dissolves either into "natural" possibility or into an uninteresting fact that our imaginations can operate without constraint. "For many more ideas can be constructed from words and images than from merely the principles and axioms on which our entire natural knowledge is based," as Spinoza noted.[14]

Logical possibility stands in need of explanation not because it is a philosophical technicality—a tricky notion to pin down—but because it relies on a notion of 'not-being-ruled-out', which in turn must provoke questions about being ruled out by what? So some context of explanation is essential, even if there is some aspiration to an absolute context: not ruled out by contradiction or by the absolute force of logic.

It must be an anachronism to think of a continuing concept of logical possibility held or used by Hume, by Leibniz, by Descartes, and so on, back to its alleged origins in Duns Scotus.[15] We can consider some views of what is possible which were explicable in terms of something other than everyday possibility (as understood at any particular time) and which may be intelligible in terms of not-being-ruled-out. What rules out impossibility, or does not rule out possibility, may vary. We can look at the variants of possibility that result from differing explanations. Whether or not this amounts to a consideration of some continuing concept of possibility or of a succession of changing concepts is not important in itself, as long as we do not think that simple comparisons between, for example, "Descartes on possibility" and "Wittgenstein on possibility" can get far without further reservations.

DESCARTES

Looking once again at the initial quotation from Descartes, the brunt of his point was that we need not care what God can do (whether or not it had some broader theological interest). What mattered was what we can do, with our natural capacities: *la finitude de l'esprit humain*, in the words of Jean-Luc Marion. Yet the theology which was pushed to one side remained fundamental beneath the surface; divine legitimation was needed to give any content to what was possible-in-principle.[16] Without it, no distinction could be sustained between (legitimated) clear conception and fallible imagination. The crux of the argument for the Real Distinction, self-evidently an important step, makes this clear: "The fact that I can clearly and distinctly understand one thing apart from another is enough to make me certain that the two things are distinct, since they are capable of being separated, at least by God."[17] ". . . at least by God" cannot be bracketed or crossed out to modernize the argument. Just from my capacity to clearly and distinctly conceive myself apart from my body it cannot follow that "the two things are distinct," for two reasons. First, the validity of my clear and distinct conception is itself underwritten only by the existence of a God with the requisite character. (This is one route into the Cartesian Circle: a deeply contentious area of exegesis. No specific resolution of the Circle need be assumed, as long as we recognise that God is not a dispensable element in it.) Second, God's support in an understanding of modality was not accidental; or rather, a nonsubjective, absolute perspective was not accidental, and no such perspective seemed persuasive without God. It was not merely Descartes's personal conviction that he could conceive his mind apart from his body. This was to be conceivable by anyone with the appropriate cognitive apparatus who judged the question in an appropriate way. One of the characteristics of secure conception in contrast with fallible imagination must have been that it was nonsubjectively reproducible; so "it is not-impossible for Descartes" must have meant just "it is not-impossible." This was the relevant difference between ordinary possibility (as in what Descartes could imagine) and the extraordinary possibility needed for the Real Distinction (what could be conceived). A nonsubjective perspective had to be assumed to maintain the difference.[18] The problem is not alleviated by pragmatic appeal, for example, to something such as "the opinion of an ideal person in similar circumstances."[19]

A parallel thought comes from the use of the evil demon at the end of the *First Meditation*. Descartes envisaged ways in which his perceptual judgments or his understanding might be mistaken. At that stage of his case it did not matter whether he had in mind his imagination or his intellection (clear and distinct conception). But then he came to consider the possibility of the suspension of his best judgment. Was it possible when using the best intellectual capacities at his command that he might be in error? He could not represent to himself how that might be so, using either his imagination or his conception. What he could suggest was how, in outline, his best capacities might err. He could not conceive this but he could portray it in a story which would offer some explanatory context. The argument depended upon a step from the natural power of his mind—the mind—to something nonnatural in the sense that it was disconnected from forms of narrative representable by him. The disconnection was essential.[20]

This two-step argument is characteristic of what came to be logical possibility. It was intrinsic to Descartes's case that his best natural endeavors could not portray to him the possible failure of his understanding. (This is another point of departure for debates over the interpretation of the Cartesian Circle.) Descartes wanted both to believe (in a sense) and to deny (in a sense) that his present conception might be in error. The equivocation was not accidental. The function of the demon (or the ad hoc hypothesis of a nonbeneficent God in the *Principles*[21]) was to offer a context for a story which was allegedly intelligible in one way but necessarily unintelligible in another. It had to make *some* sense that the demon might be at work. Richard Popkin has explained the historical context from the witch trials of the 1630s.[22] But equally, the machinery of the demon's workings had to be obscure. If they could be understood transparently ("clearly and distinctly") then their use as a source of possible error would be neutralized, which is to say that the possibility would lose its force or content.

There are many controversial points here, but the only one relevant to this argument should be the need for the step from the ordinary possibility of what Descartes could imagine or conceive to the extraordinary possibility where he could represent only its possible existence (God or the demon might be deceiving him now), not its coherent detail. The use of possibility in this, one of his foundational arguments, depended once again on some nonsubjective perspective or form of representation. Again, given his assumptions, some form of theology was not optional. A step beyond the natural was required to maintain his case. And at that point, the step was one he should not have been licensed to take, by his own standards.

HUME

A psychological slant in Hume's approach has been seen by almost every commentator. Apparently, no connection was explained or justified between a capacity to imagine the movements of billiard balls and what is actually possible on a billiard table. I can assert, for example, that *my* imagination only allows me to envisage situations that accord with causal laws. I can even assert, narrow-mindedly, that I cannot imagine anyone else imagining things differently. Such feeble personal considerations would prove as much or as little as Hume's appeals to his own mental capacities. Arthur Pap, in one much-cited discussion, wrote of Hume's "absurd identification of the logically possible with the imaginable," diagnosing fallacy, error, and confusion all on a single page.[23] In fact, it seems quite likely that what mattered to Hume was the explanation for his degree of belief in possibilities, rather than their objective ontological status, in which case it might be useful to redirect our attention from his seeming psychologism to his central modal logic, which has received far less discussion.

A philosopher who accepts some form of a principle of sufficient reason may have some basis for saying that something is possible: there is no cause or reason why it should not be so. What, though, could have been Hume's support for his use of a notion of possibility? How could he have been in a position to assume that anything might be metaphysically possible (or, in fact, possible at all in any noncircular sense) because he could not think of a reason why it should not be so? How could metaphysical possibility—or absolute availability—be assumed as part of a critique of alleged knowledge of metaphysical necessity? A wide, nonstandard concept of possibility is, after all, at least as much in need of justification as any notion of causal necessity; perhaps rather more so ("there is as good reason for taking everything to be impossible, as to be possible . . ."[24]). The reader might suspect that Hume intended irony in referring to "an establish'd maxim in metaphysics"—"*whatever the mind clearly conceives includes the idea of possible existence* or in other words, *that nothing we imagine is absolutely impossible*"—but it seems that he did not.[25] It takes little to persuade me to believe that the sun (in one sense) must rise tomorrow, but surely rather more to persuade me to even suppose that (in any sense) it might not. A supporter of the force of natural law might have some justification for identifying causal or explanatory availability with possibility. Hume was as entitled as anyone to make use of the concept of being not-self-contradictory, but he had less justification than anyone for identifying this concept with possibility of any kind. To do this would be to beg the question by assuming that what can happen would be what is not ruled out by contradiction. But what would be the force in *not ruled out* here, and from what context would it derive its sense? If the sense was the same as *logically available*, then this would be uncontroversial, but also unhelpful or even useless for any purpose he might intend.

Here is a typical Humean argument:

> as all distinct ideas are separable from each other, and as the ideas of cause and effect are evidently distinct, 'twill be easy for us to conceive any object to be nonexistent this moment, and existent the next, without conjoining to it the distinct idea of cause or productive principle. The separation, therefore, of the idea of a cause from that of a beginning of existence, is plainly possible for the imagination; and consequently the actual separation of these objects is so far possible, that it implies no contradiction nor absurdity; and is therefore incapable of being refuted by any reasoning from mere ideas; without which 'tis impossible to demonstrate the necessity of a cause.[26]

The important step is from the separation which is "plainly possible for the imagination" to the possibility of an "actual separation." The obvious, superficial difficulty in the use of Hume's imagination masks the more fundamental logical problem of identifying any kind of possibility with that which "implies no contradiction nor absurdity." The reality was that Hume had nothing solid to support the notion of possibility he assumed. He must have wanted his readers to think that the "actual separation" could happen in some sense; after all, what else could "actual" imply? Taken for granted in his argument was a principle that anything can happen unless there is a reason why it should not (a principle with clear echoes in his social philosophy and his views on free will). Yet he could have no justification for accepting that principle. There are excellent reasons why two billiard balls do not stop dead on collision. To claim that in any sense they might not stop dead—that there are not sufficient reasons why they should not—was either straightforwardly false or was to apply a less stringent standard to what is not ruled out by reason than the standard applied to what reason is assumed to allow or support.

There are contexts in which a notion of what is 'not unallowable' may be useful. But any identification of such a notion with a notion of 'what can happen' needs some justification. A body of natural law might aim to provide one kind of justification (but obviously not for Hume). More plausibly nowadays, a body of scientific theory may be hoped to provide another. What can happen in nature may be identified with what is allowed (or not excluded) by the terms of a theory, although it must be doubtful whether such a view could be defended beyond a pragmatic level.

The superficial similarity in logic between Descartes and Hume is misleading. The argument for the Real Distinction, once again, says that "the fact that I can clearly and distinctly understand one thing apart from another is enough to make me certain that the two things are distinct, since they are capable of being separated, at least by God." That sounds not unlike Hume's "the separation . . . of the idea of a cause from that of a beginning of existence, is plainly possible for the imagination; and consequently the actual separation of these objects is so far possible, that it implies no contradiction nor absurdity." The common form is: I can represent . . . to myself, so . . . is possible. The supports beneath the use of that form were not the same for Hume as for Descartes, but they did share one significant feature: they rested on assumptions that should not have been used at the stage of the argument where they were used. For Descartes, God's perspective was not an optional extra: it could be modernized into an absolute, objectivized conception but not eliminated from the argument altogether.

Certainly, Hume wanted to dispense with theological assumptions. His hope may have been to use possibility at what might now be called a logical level: his separation of objects was possible in that "it implies no contradiction nor absurdity." One problem was in the step from (loosely) *not*

ruled out (by logic) to *possible*, as just discussed. Another, as noted, on the surface, was his psychologism: why should we care what he was able to imagine? A more fundamental difficulty was his use of representation, putting to
one side the fact that the representation he favored was psychological, veer-
ing painfully close to mental picturing. To understand that a separation of
objects "implies no contradiction nor absurdity," Hume had to represent the
separation to himself. The logic in the passage quoted earlier from his
Abstract was oblique: "The mind can always *conceive* any effect to follow
from any cause, and indeed any event to follow upon another: whatever we
conceive is possible, at least in a metaphysical sense: but wherever a demonstration takes place, the contrary is impossible, and implies a contradiction."
We might think that the latter part of this—"wherever a demonstration
takes place . . ."—was independent from, and stronger than, the first part—
"whatever we *conceive* is possible. . . ." But that is not so. We have to conceive—represent to ourselves—the possible existence of "the contrary."
Here, Hume was not far from Descartes. To get any useful inference from
"I can represent . . . to myself," some nonsubjective understanding was
required: ". . . can be represented . . . is representable." Unlike Descartes,
Hume might have wanted to appeal to the representational capacities of the
ordinary, rational person rather than to the eye of God. But still, "can be
represented" would have to be taken as "can be represented by somebody,
in principle." (This is so whether we regard his intentions towards causality
as being essentially critical or as a constructive account grounded in Human
Nature.) One might wonder how far that sort of implied understanding
relied upon a religious past to give it legitimacy. And still the important difficulties would remain: what was the plausible connection between repre-
sentability-in-principle and any valuable sense of possibility? A link could
be made by definition; but why should such a definition be accepted?

THE TRACTATUS

Hume relied upon an indeterminate notion of representability to maintain
his belief in an idea of what was possible, or not ruled out, "at least in a
metaphysical sense." His only systematic support could have been some
back-door assumption, along the lines that an absolute or nonsubjective
conception owed its legitimacy (or rather, plausibility) to some recollection
of a divine perspective.

   The link between representation and possibility reached its clearest
extreme in Wittgenstein's *Tractatus*. There, the link was direct, but not in the

manner of psychological empiricism, despite the apparent parallel between
"What can be described can also happen . . ." [6.362] and Hume's "whatever we *conceive* is possible." When Wittgenstein wrote that "Thought can
never be of anything illogical . . ." [3.03] he was not saying anything either
for or against the traditional empiricists' thought-experiment to test for the
presence of logical possibility. The linkage in the *Tractatus* was not between
possibility and psychological representation or the capacity of our imaginations (or alleged intellection) but between possibility and sense. Paul Engelmann emphasized how thoroughly the psychological was purged:

> One of the very few corrections written by hand into the original
> typescript of the *Tractatus* deletes the decisive sentence "We conceive
> facts in pictures" ["Die Tatsachen begreifen wir in Bildern"], and sub-
> stitutes "We make for ourselves pictures of the facts." ["Wir machen
> wir uns Bilder der Tatsachen" 2.1][27]

What was possible was what could be said. What was said was what was
possible: this itself could not be said, but only shown. Plainly, this was the
important part of what Wittgenstein meant in stating that what can be
described can also happen: the fact of representation was the fact that something was possible.

The medium of representation came to be not the mind but the
proposition. A proposition (true or false) showed a possible state of affairs.
The proposition was the unit of (possible) sense. "A proposition *shows* its
sense. A proposition *shows* how things stand *if* it is true. And it *says that* they
do so stand." [4.022] It was able to do this because it was in essence a picture. The picturing—representational—capacity of the proposition derived
its legitimacy from the presumption that language works: we do convey
sense to each other. We do that by means of propositions, true or false. Sense
in language—the fact that we make sense—depended on the sense made
by propositions. We could not make sense, convey truth, or understand each
other unless language rested upon the picturing of possible states of affairs
by propositions. "The possibility of propositions is based on the principle
that objects have signs as their representatives." [4.0312]

So possibility was seen in two different ways. The possibility *in* a proposition was simply enough the fact that it was a proposition. Here, a possible
state of affairs was one which could be pictured—conveyed successfully as
sense. "A picture contains the possibility of the situation that it represents."
[2.203] There was also the possibility *of* propositions, which must have been
a transcendental possibility propped up by a characteristically two-way

transcendental conditional: propositions were (possible) portrayals of sense because "objects have signs as their representatives"; signs must represent objects because "If the world had no substance, then whether a proposition had sense would depend on whether another proposition was true." [2.0211] Wittgenstein said nothing about transcendental possibility in the *Tractatus* (nor would he have described it in that way), no doubt because it would fall plainly into the category of the showable rather than the sayable or describable. The picturing relationship itself, and hence the fact that a proposition pictures a state of affairs, was not picturable: "A picture cannot . . . depict its pictorial form: it displays it." [2.172][28]

The *Tractatus* matters because it offered the clearest account of logical possibility, brought unambiguously into identity with the possibility in logic, itself brought unambiguously into identity with the possibility of what we can or cannot think. ("A thought contains the possibility of the situation of which it is the thought. What is thinkable is possible too." [3.02]) At the time of writing the *Tractatus*, Wittgenstein had no overt interest in any notion of everyday, commonplace possibility. He used a negative form of expression—"The only impossibility that exists is *logical* impossibility" [6.375]—which suggests that the only possibility that exists is logical possibility. Whether or not that was so, we can be certain that he was not concerned about changing the way we speak. Our language is in order as it is [5.5563]. He was not even concerned about what makes possible, in the sense of transcendental conditions, "our" use of normal modalities. (You can understand "I could be in Los Angeles today" because, in some way—there is some world in which—I am, or possibly-am, in Los Angeles.) Rather, he was interested in the absolute force of logical impossibility and in the fact that sense relies on the portrayal of possible states of affairs [3.3421].

Nevertheless, there remained an analogy between his views and the most straightforward appeal to the powers of the mind. Compare:

Euphranor: Pray, Alciphron, which are those things you would call absolutely impossible?

Alciphron: Such as include a contradiction.

Euphranor: Can you frame an idea of what includes a contradiction?

Alciphron: I cannot.

Euphranor: Consequently, whatever is absolutely impossible you cannot form an idea of?

Alciphron: This I grant.

Here, for Berkeley, to "frame" or "form" an idea was exactly analogous to the expression of sense, that is, just expression, for Wittgenstein. The force of the impossibility was the veto of the unthinkable: you are simply not able, he said, to form certain ideas (and for Berkeley, specifically, there could be no question of any state of affairs distinct from the idea someone formed of it).[29] The force of impossibility for Wittgenstein must have been the threatened breakdown of sense. If it were, per impossibile, possible to portray, or convey in language, an impossible state of affairs, then the communication of truth and falsity could not operate and sense would collapse. (Any parallel with Berkeley breaks down significantly here. Alciphron was arguing that theological discourse could be used meaningfully when no representable ideas could be in the mind.)

For the early Wittgenstein, the connections between possible thought, logical thought, and logical possibility were intimate. He would have derided any notion of logic as the laws of thought, or rational thought, in a psychological sense. Yet anything that was to qualify as a thought would have to be expressible, hence to be a proposition, hence to have sense,[30] hence to picture a possible state of affairs. Logical impossibility would be excluded as *sinnlos*, senseless. Also excluded would be *Unsinn*, the nonsense that derived from attempts to say the unsayable, portray depiction, or, as we might put it, enunciate the transcendental conditions of sense.

WITTGENSTEIN: LATER POSSIBILITIES

The real difficulty in all this emerged as Wittgenstein's thinking developed after 1929. The fault line created by the color-exclusion problem was discussed exhaustively in the 1930s as a question about necessity. In fact, in his own words, the issue was one of impossibility: the simultaneous presence of two colors was "logically impossible." [6.3751] The development of his views on possibility and impossibility has been far less well studied.

The survival of any sort of logical possibility into his later works might seem surprising. He did say in the *Philosophical Grammar* that a "question about absolute possibility" is "always nonsense";[31] but there, as elsewhere, his understanding of mathematical (and particularly geometrical) possibility may have constrained the apparently inexorable line of his thinking. We might expect him to have believed that logical possibility is an archetypal philosophers' invention. In fact, his later attitude seems to have been more ambivalent than on almost any other topic. We see a blurring between possibility and logical possibility: "There are cases where doubt is unreasonable, but others where it seems logically impossible. And there seems to be no clear boundary between them." "We are not made aware of how various the employment of the assertion ". . . is possible . . ." is!"[32] In places he adopted a startlingly realist-sounding tone: an analogy between logical possibility and chemical possibility suggests powerfully that modality belongs unequivocally in things and not in how we talk or think about them. Much of his thinking in the notes published as the *Remarks on the Foundations of Mathematics* may have been intended to suggest both a blurred spectrum or family of cases and some analogy with practical, almost mechanical possibility.[33]

More often, though, there are signs of a different-looking approach: "We tend to think of a possibility as something in nature . . ." he said in the *Yellow Book*, and he ended his case by saying "We have the idea that we are putting up a standard of usage in nature, but in fact we are only putting up a standard of usage in grammar." Or "One might even say that philosophy is the grammar of the words *must* and *can*, for that is how it shows what is a priori and what a posteriori."[34] Discussing the possibility of trisecting an angle in the *Philosophical Grammar*, he said that "The question whether trisection is possible is . . . the question whether there is such a thing in the game as trisection." In his 1934–1935 lectures, leaving apparently almost no room for finer shades of interpretation: "The essence of logical possibility is what is laid down in language," and "To talk about logical possibility is to talk about a rule for expressions." And once again, in the *Yellow Book*, going back to the subject which had caused him so much trouble and which was filling the pages of philosophical journals through the 1930s, he asked, "When we say a thing cannot be green and yellow at the same time we are excluding something, but what?" The reply was that "We have not excluded any case at all, but rather the use of an expression."[35]

It is pointless to weigh up any realist-versus-idealist or conceptualist strains in his later approaches to logical possibility (does it reside in the world or in us?). On this point, Anscombe's otherwise cautious discussion seems to lose focus. Writing about *Investigations*, section 521, on chemical possibility, she says that the exclusion of a chemical or logical possibility "belongs to the system, a human construction. It is objective; that is, it is not for me to decide what is allowable here."[36] That only transfers logical possibility from me and how I talk to us and how we talk, which in theoretical terms may be no more than a shift from idealism to conceptualism. It does not do much for someone inclined to think that it is something about space that prevents the trisection of an angle with a straight-edge and compasses or about water and sand that prevents them from mixing. How are chemical properties human constructions? "The syntax of reality and possibility" does not help a lot.[37]

The fact is, though, that any imagined opposition between modal realism and nonrealism must be out of place in considering how Wittgenstein saw his thinking. If a label is needed for his view, it could be *transcendental naturalism*.[38] His position remained transcendental because it still contained the double conditional characteristic of transcendental arguments: the logical possibilities embodied in the grammar of our language were there because things were like that, *and* things were seen like that because of the construction of logical possibilities in the grammar of our language. To think about the use of language "creating" modalities or modalities in reality "determining" the framework of language is to miss the two-way double dependence. We think of naturalism because things indeed are like that, not otherwise, as seen in the example from *On Certainty*: "A principal ground for Moore to assume that he was never on the moon is that no one was ever on the moon or *could* ever come there; and this we believe on grounds of what we learn."[39] The *could* might be logical or not; it is as absolute as nature requires.

What is important—and the reason for dwelling on Wittgenstein's later views—is that a link was retained between possibility and making sense. Going back to the remarks about chemical possibility in the 1939 lectures: "When you say 'H_2O_4 is possible' you simply mean it as a sign in your system. . . . We have adopted a language in which it *makes sense* to say 'H_2O_4 . . .'—it isn't true, but it makes sense." More centrally, in the middle of the private language passages in the *Investigations*: "In so far as it makes *sense* [Soweit es Sinn hat] to say that my pain is the same as his, it is also possible for us [soweit können wir auch] both to have the same pain."[40]

It is improbable that Wittgenstein could ever have accepted a position as stark as the caricature in Waismann's *Principles of Linguistic Philosophy*:

> One meaning of "possible" of particular importance is obtained when the rules involved are those of logical grammar. In this case we will speak of "logical possibility." That water should run uphill is physically impossible, but logically possible. The criterion for whether a state of affairs is logically possible is whether the sentence which describes it makes sense.[41]

More likely, he was too sensible to believe that it was possible that water should run uphill in any way whatever. His link between logical possibility and sense cannot have been so crude, but it did contain great difficulties.

The tendency in his later work was entirely against any theoretical essence of meaning—any set of conditions that might determine what makes sense. In the *Tractatus*, the "essence of all description" was given in the "essence of a proposition" or "the general propositional form": "This is how things stand" [Es verhält sich so und so, 5.4711, 5.471, 4.5]. Later, this was not seen as wrong so much as "the same as giving the definition: a proposition is whatever can be true or false." But the nature of a proposition, even if created or defined, could reveal nothing about the essence of making sense.[42]

Yet possibility and making sense were directly connected through Wittgenstein's naturalism. In his *Philosophical Remarks*, referring to Mach, he noted, "a thought-experiment is of course not an experiment at all. At bottom it is a grammatical investigation." And in any case, what is not imaginable may be what I "declare" to be unimaginable.[43] His view must have been that what is possible (in a broad, logical interpretation, if we want to add this) will be what it makes sense to say, and that will depend on the fabric of the language in which it is said, which in turn will depend on a scaffolding of "certain very general facts of nature": "It is as if our concepts involved a scaffolding of facts." That would presumably mean: If you imagine certain facts otherwise, describe them otherwise, than the way they are, then you can no longer imagine the application of certain concepts. . . . All this was more fragile that it might seem. In the *Yellow Book*, he said: "It is queer that we should say what it is that is impossible, e.g., that the mantel piece cannot be yellow and green at the same time. In speaking of that which is impossible it seems as though we are conceiving the inconceivable."[44]

His conclusion was that "what we exclude has no semblance of sense." This is curious—maybe it was just rhetoric—because that is actually the real difficulty: there is a genuine *semblance* of sense in many such cases. Why have philosophers wasted their time on discussions about the possibility of time travel or artificial intelligence if these projects contained no semblance of sense? The treatment could not be said to be satisfactory (and these arguments did not recur in writings intended for eventual publication). Wittgenstein went on to say that "we exclude such sentences as 'It is both green and yellow' because we do not want to use them," and then he added, cagily, "Of course we *could* give these sentences sense."

The color example was well chosen, in that it might have helped his presumed point. His difficulty was that what he said was hard to apply where logical impossibilities may apparently be used with sense. "Is it a genuine question if we ask whether it's possible to trisect an angle?"[45] Here was the real trouble, as seen in Wittgenstein's own questions in the *Philosophical Grammar:* "If the trisection of an angle is impossible—logically impossible—how can we ask questions about it at all? How can we describe what is logically impossible and significantly raise the question of its possibility?"[46] The emphasis should be on how we can *describe* what is logically impossible, because no one doubts that we can ask whether, or suppose that, or tell someone falsely it is possible to trisect an angle with a ruler and compass. And here the trouble was of Wittgenstein's own making. He was caught both ways. If we can "describe what is logically impossible," then his notion of logical impossibility loses its only support: severed successfully from unimaginability, it has to rest solely on a relationship with making sense, with what can be said. If we can not describe what is logically impossible, then Wittgenstein's broad, nontheoretical account of sense seems to be undermined. On what basis, after all, could he say that an apparently well-formed, intelligible description could not make sense to someone? (Interestingly, Drury recounted a conversation with Wittgenstein in 1929 in which he reported a comment by W. E. Johnson: "If I say that a sentence has meaning for me, no one has a right to say it is senseless."[47])

In so far as he retained any concept of logical possibility—even as an extreme case, with blurred edges—he may have been resting it, as much as in the *Tractatus*, on making sense. Where "a combination of words is being excluded from the language,"[48] this may be because it has no use. Or rather we want to say *can have* no use, but that would beg the question and at the same time go against Wittgenstein's naturalism. Once sense was severed from the conditions that supported it in the *Tractatus*, it could no longer sustain a form of possibility or impossibility that could be used with any sort of critical force.

The upshot was that logical possibility would have been stranded philosophically. Suppose, for example, someone were to conduct a "grammatical investigation" into time travel. Superficially, one might come to a conclusion that time travel is impossible (*logically* adds nothing here) because of contradictions that would soon crop up with "our" normal discourse (e.g., "I was living before my father")—apparent nonsense. Wittgenstein would not accept that simplistic approach. His view might be that "our" language about time gets its sense from its use in relation to what we know about time, that much (but not all) of what we now know excludes time travel, that (for all we know) further discoveries may produce developments in the grammar of our language, and so forth. The conclusion from that plausible line of thought is that logical possibility ceases to matter. What can be said ("with sense") depends to some degree on how things are, which particle physicists will tell us in due course.

That is as far as we need to go with Wittgenstein. He might not regard such comments as being critically negative, especially since they tend to subvert any pretensions towards a distinctly logical possibility under the guardianship of philosophers. Nevertheless, from the point of view of the exegesis of his later work we can see that a deep ambivalence remained. If, for example, geometrical impossibility is somehow a matter of grammar, which is somehow related to how things are in geometry, we can still press the question whether the "game" does or does not depend upon how things are—how space is.[49] Any plausible answers he might give will look unhelpful. It can be said that geometrical possibility is identifiable with availability or deducibility within a certain set of Hilbertian axioms, but that sort of possibility could never be projectible by analogy into a wider field, of ordinary sense, for example. Or it could be said that geometrical possibility relates in some way, however vaguely, to what can actually be done with a compass, straightedge and pencil. Perhaps an impossibility proof for trisection could be seen as an extreme case of innumerable, failed trisection experiments. Or as a kind of rule excluding such experiments. However plausible that might be, even in a far more sophisticated formulation,[50] it would equate possibility with practicability in a way which would give it no critical value in any wider context of discourse. Again, that could have been Wittgenstein's intention.

LOGICAL IMPOSSIBILITY?

The discussion may seem to have missed a crucial point. Logical impossibility might not be ruled out by divine sanction, or by what we cannot conceive, or by what we cannot express, but it can be ruled out, of course, by logic.

In a sense, that cannot be wrong, but it can be circular. In a Diodoran conditional, for example, *if P, then Q* could be read as *it is not possible that P and not-Q*. Circularly, then, the possibility of *P and not-Q* will be "ruled out by logic" simply enough, because the force of logic would be the same as the force of Diodoran possibility (which had to be understood in a temporal way). Or in constructivist terms, *P and not-P* may (or may not) be excluded by the force of whatever rule, convention, policy, or decision is favored. Logical impossibility might then be intelligible in terms of such exclusion. The point in both cases is that some context of exclusion is required.

This leads to paradox. Logical impossibility, on most readings, must be strongly excluding: the logically impossible has to be completely ruled out. Being ruled out within some specified context—the psychological context of what I can imagine, or a context of an axiomatized geometry, or within an agreed physical theory—will be reasonably unproblematic. But there may be two difficulties. First, the problem about many contexts of interest to philosophers is that they are not closed or well defined. An alleged context of *what we say*, for example, could never license useful inferences from local to wider impossibility. If we are debating, for example, whether the soul can (possibly) exist apart from the body, then the context of possibility is not at all obvious: within some frameworks of thought it might sound possible, in others not. Which leads to a second problem: that we may be hoping for a non-context-bound, absolute concept of possibility, where the impossible is ruled out not only in one context or in some contexts or even in all, but in all possible contexts. Taking the same example, the ambition (or pretension) might be to show that the separate existence of the soul is not just impossible if one thinks or talks in a certain way, but is completely impossible, absolutely ruled out. The paradox is that a sort of possibility which might apply within specified contexts will aspire to apply in all contexts. If the context is what enforces the possibility, then this looks like a big obstacle.

In historical terms, the progression towards some absolute context of representation seems to be tidy. We begin the story with appeals to God's representations, then slide towards the representational capacities of our minds, then try a more general concept of a proposition as a medium of representation, and then, perhaps, resort to pure logic. Parts of this story are variants of conventional philosophical narratives, from Foucault and Rorty.[51]

An omission from the story is Leibniz, with his modern admirers. Surely we can find a neutral supporting context for a strong form of impossibility in the notion of falsity in all possible worlds? Surely such a notion supports the invaluable step from one particular context to any context, evading any hazards of local context-dependence?

It could be as well to leave the historical Leibniz aside, because his possibility-in-possible-worlds was even more tinged with theological assumptions than any view of Descartes. For him, it was essential, not incidental, that it was possible for God to create worlds in certain ways. His thinking on possibility was formed in explicit response to problems about divine choice. It can be reduced to near nonsense when taken outside that context.[52] But a modernized view of possible worlds may still seem helpful. And so it may be, in some ways, though the point at issue now is not so much one of semantics as one of legitimation. Our question is not whether any model theory is feasible for formal modal systems, or whether any modal systems have better or worse standing in relation to informal modal discourse. We need make no assumptions about the order of priority between the informal and the formal. The level of concern must be far more primitive.

There need be no problem with impossibility related to extremely wide or vague contexts, even to contexts we scarcely know how to specify. A physicist without any comprehensive characterization of a physical theory can still feel relaxed about relying on some notion of physical impossibility.[53] Such casual pragmatism would be far more awkward in a logical context. Certainly, a confidence in logical impossibility could seem alarming in the absence of some agreed characterization of logic. If we mean, unambiguously, *a* logic, in the sense of a formal system, then there is no problem; but that will only give us a trick with mirrors. If we mean *any possible* logic, we may be heading for circularity. The whole force of logical impossibility, and hence the appeal of logical possibility, cannot apply only within any context or system. An appeal to a wider context is obligatory, yet it must be as self-defeating as a relativist's attachment to the absolute persuasiveness of the relativity of truth or rationality.

The existence (in some sense) of possible worlds may (or may not) provide a descriptive model for the use of language about possibilities or counterfactuals (such a loose formulation will allow scope for innumerable refinements). One might entertain the general idea, with Michael Loux, that "possible worlds are elements in the ontology to which we commit ourselves in our nonphilosophical discourse."[54] Yet to think about conditions for the use of "our" language about possibilities—our "commitments"—would be to endow models of possible worlds with an illegitimate legitimizing power. The assumption would be that our uses of possibilities in "our" language are governed by some conditions about how things are: unless the world was like that, we could not talk like this . . . ; we could not make sense to each other unless. . . . Here, *governed* and *could not* would be transcendental, and hence question-begging.

≈

This chapter has not aimed to contradict any understanding of logical possibility, except a view that it can be understood with no explanatory

context. A discontinuous history has been marshalled to show how supporting contexts can be unstable. Past aspirations may well have been to find
some theatre of representation which was both beyond normal imagining
and at the same time accessible as a source of endorsement or legitimation.
In so far as we can draw any conclusion across history, it might be that later
versions of metaphysical, conceptual, or logical possibility exploited the
force of a notion derived from a divine perspective while ignoring or deny-
ing any theological presuppositions. A wide notion of possibility in a sense
of *what God can do* may be perfectly satisfactory where the supporting context is accepted. Divine power, after all, should provide the most solid form
of legitimation for those who accept it. Before Leibniz, this can be seen well
in al-Ghazâli: "that which is not impossible is within power."[55] We may
wonder how far subsequent concepts of absolute representation—in the
mind, in language, or in logic—were shadows of that earlier view.

A notion of a limit or veto to what cannot be thought (or expressed
or represented) must play some part in any view about where logic starts—
not only modal logic, but logic in as much as it may need to characterise
the prohibitive force of inconsistency.

Caution about totalization or closure has been a familiar theme in philosophy right up to the present. Graham Priest has given an historical and
analytical survey from Plato to Derrida. A more austere treatment has been
given by Patrick Grim. More darkly, this was a central theme in the work
of Emmanuel Levinas.[56] The clearest and best-known enunciation of a limit
[Grenze] to what can be thought was in the assertive Preface to Wittgenstein's *Tractatus*:

> the aim of the book is to set a limit to thought, or rather—not to
> thought, but to the expression of thoughts: for in order to be able to set
> a limit to thought, we should have to find both sides of the limit think-
> able (i.e., we should have to be able to think what cannot be thought).
>
> It will therefore only be in language that the limit can be set, and what
> lies on the other side of the limit will simply be nonsense.

We have seen how intimately the limits to the expression of thoughts (as
propositions) were connected with possibility. What seems surprising is that
Wittgenstein made no use of the distinction used by Kant: "Boundaries
[Grenzen] (in extended things) always presuppose a space that is found outside a certain fixed location, and that encloses that location; limits
[Schranken] require nothing of the kind, but are mere negations that affect
a magnitude insofar as it does not possess absolute completeness. . . ."[57]

Wittgenstein saw the problem in a boundary: "we should have to be able to think what cannot be thought"—"both sides." The difficulty with a limit is one of totalization. To assert that no possible car can travel at more than 1000 miles per hour calls for some characterization of a possible car which need only be as strong as the strength of possibility required (and this could vary). But if there can be no totality of ideas, or representations, or thoughts, or propositions, then the characterization of a possible idea or representation, and so on, will not be reliable. This is why the infinite power of God was so helpful in the past; why logical possibility is so helpless when God disappears.

CHAPTER 2

THE TRUTH IN WHAT WE SAY

In a manuscript from around 1926, F. P. Ramsey wrote:

> One source of . . . confusion must be eliminated straight away; besides
> the primary meaning in which we apply it to statements or opinions,
> the word *true* can also be used in a number of derived and metaphori-
> cal senses which it is no part of our problem to discuss. Obscure utter-
> ances such as "Beauty is truth, truth beauty" we shall make no attempts
> to elucidate, and confine ourselves to the plain work-a-day sense in
> which it is true that Charles I was beheaded and that the earth is round.[1]

Elsewhere, he noted tersely that "Truth and falsity are ascribed primarily to propositions." This helped to clear the ground for his demonstration that "there is really no separate problem of truth but merely a linguistic muddle."[2]

From the same time, but in an entirely different manner, Heidegger
wrote:

> The thesis that the genuine "locus" of truth is the judgment not only
> invokes Aristotle unjustly, it also fails with regard to its content to rec-
> ognize the structure of truth. The statement is not the primary "locus"
> of truth, but *the other way round*, the statement as a mode of appropri-
> ation of discoveredness and as a way of being-in-the-world is based in
> discovering, or in the *disclosedness* of Da-sein. The most primordial
> "truth" is the "locus" of the statement and the ontological condition
> of the possibility that statements can be true or false (discovering or
> covering over).[3]

One natural thought might be that here we see not so much a complete opposition as a difference of interests. Ramsey's assumption that he could approach truth in terms of the truth of propositions, statements, or opinions was extremely typical of philosophical logicians looking for a safely noncontroversial starting point. He did not deny that truth has other interpretations, although he did believe that these were "derived and metaphorical." Despite Heidegger's explicit disagreement with that view, we might imagine that his own position might be marginal to any progress in logic. Even he, we might hope, would see that when we want to discuss "the general conception of logic as the science of rational thought,"[4] in Ramsey's words, we can take for granted a focused, propositional understanding of truth, if only for the sake of useful argument. The exclusion of other, less "plain" senses might miss some interesting color but would cost nothing in relevance or importance.

This chapter argues a diametrically opposite view. The narrowing of discussions of truth into discussions of true propositions (statements, sentences) excludes everything which makes truth intelligible and valuable. Ramsey's ordering of plain and metaphorical senses was upside down. It is the understanding of truth as propositional which is derivative, from a wider interpretation. It is truth-as-true-propositions which can be seen as metaphor, relying on images of representation and correspondence, even where these may be repudiated explicitly, as they were by Ramsey himself. Problems in the definition of truth originate by stripping away everything that makes truth valuable so that there is nothing left to characterize it. Frege noted: "The word *true* specifies the goal. Logic is concerned with the predicate *true* in a special way. The word *true* characterizes logic. *True* cannot be defined. . . ."[5] The train of association in his remarks was causal, although Frege would certainly not agree to that himself: because he thought "Logic is concerned with the predicate *true* in a special way," it turned out that "*True* cannot be defined." Further, and worse, logical difficulties in the handling of truth are connected with the very first choices made in an approach to it. What seems to be a pragmatic attitude is in fact the source of the trouble it seeks to evade. We may want to believe that the choice made explicitly by Ramsey— to confine himself to "plain work-a-day" truth—if not unavoidable, was pragmatic, in that without it he could get nowhere. The case here is the converse: *with* that choice we get into trouble.

That is not to say that Ramsey was wrong and Heidegger was right, as if there were some agreed ground on which they could have differed. They may have been on the same ground, but they were travelling over it in different ways.

Part of Heidegger's case was historical or etymological. As in the passage quoted above, he felt that the origin of truth in early Greek philosophy—in what he saw as a notion of discoveredness or disclosedness—was significant. The point, repeated throughout his work, must have been that some valuable nonpropositional or prepropositional sense of truth had evaporated. He believed that the crucial choice had been in the connection made by Plato in the *Sophist* between truth and falsity and *logos*, in preference to an earlier association between truth and existence.[6] Yet a purely historical case would be hard to make in a way that would give any logical leverage: "Back to Parmenides" may be an amusing slogan, but it is baffling as a practical prescription. The etymological case is equally doubtful. Alexander Mourelatos mentions "a certain theory, first proposed by Heidegger and now favored by a number of German scholars," in which "*alêtheia* is a mode of being which qualifies and enhances things directly, independently of a relationship of adequacy or correspondence between the 'true things' and their representation. . . ." All this, he believes, was too strong to be supported by the linguistic facts of Greek usage.[7] Heidegger did not pursue a Homeric version of truth in a sense of trustworthy reporting which would seem to be more interesting than intimations of *Unverborgenheit* or disclosedness.

His case was not only historical. Near the beginning of his treatment of truth in *Being and Time*, he referred to Kant's verdict at the opening of the Transcendental Dialectic: "Truth and illusion are not in the object insofar as it is intuited, but in the judgment about it insofar as it is thought." Or, in his own words, "the ideal content of judgment" may be held to "stand in a relation of agreement" with a real thing. "How," he asked, "is the relation between an ideal being and a real thing objectively present to be grasped ontologically?" Then, tellingly, "Is not the reality of knowing and judging sundered into two kinds of being, two 'levels' that can never be pieced together so as to get the kind of being of knowing?" The conclusion he wanted to reach was that "truth by no means has the structure of an agreement between knowing and the object in the sense of a correspondence of one being (subject) to another (object)."[8] He may have been right in thinking that he was digging up presuppositions that would lie beneath any view of truth as correspondence, but the point he touched was a more general one. Even, as for example in Ramsey's case, where correspondence was repudiated, there might remain some relation between the content of what was thought or asserted and what was so in reality. For Heidegger, the basic difficulty lay in the "sundering" of knowing and existence into "two kinds of being, two 'levels' that can never be pieced together." If we imagine that the real problem of truth is in a relation between judgments or propositions or words and reality, then we may already have made a distinction which is going to make our problem insoluble. Such thinking has to be suggestive rather than conclusive. It is strangely in harmony with Ramsey's laconic insight:

> . . . supposing for a moment that only one form of proposition is in question, say the relational form *aRb*; then "He is always right" could be expressed by "For all *a, R, b,* if he asserts *aRb,* then *aRb,*" to which "is true" would be an obviously superfluous addition. When all forms of proposition are included, the analysis is more complicated but not essentially different; and it is clear that the problem is not as to the nature of truth and falsehood, but as to the nature of judgment or assertion, for what is difficult to analyse in the above formulation is "He asserts *aRb*."[9]

Whatever the details of history or etymology, no one doubts that the associations of truth must lie in telling, asserting or trusting. It is "part of the concept of truth that we aim at making true statements," writes Dummett. But what of the remaining part of the concept, and which part matters? He has told us that "the notion of truth is born in the first place, out of less specific modes of commendation of an assertoric utterance, from the necessity to distinguish between it and the epistemic notion of justifiability . . ."[10] which may be so; but how much of the point or sense or value of truth derives from the "less specific modes of commendation," and how much is lost when we focus on the more specific?

THE VALUE OF TRUTH

Restarting from a wholly different perspective, here is a view from Iris Murdoch:

> "Truth" is found by "truthful" endeavor, both words are needed in a just description of language. Truth is learnt, found, in specialized areas of art where the writer (for instance) struggles to make his deep intuitions of the world into artful truthful judgment. This is the truth, terrible, delightful, funny, whose strong lively presence we recognize in great writers and whose absence we feel in the weak, self-regarding fantasy of bad writers. The world is not given to us "on a plate," it is given to us as a creative task. It is impossible to banish morality from this picture. We *work,* using or failing to use our honesty, our courage, our truthful imagination, at the interpretation of what is present to us, as we of necessity shape it and "make something of it." We help it to be.[11]

She was making a case against an undervaluing of truth by philosophers whom she classified as "structuralists." Hence her need to explain why truth matters. One way to say why truth matters is to insist that it really exists, against theorists who may seem to claim that it does not, or that it exists only partially or relatively. In a different way, that was the line taken at the beginning of the twentieth century by Russell and Moore against pragmatism, and against an understanding of degrees of truth which they saw in Bradley. Moore, for example, was confident that "*some* facts are facts, and *some* truths true, which never have been, are not now, and never will be experienced *at all*, and which are not timelessly experienced either."[12] Russell changed his mind many times on the nature of truth, but he never abandoned his conviction that truth was morally important. Partial truth, or truth relativized, would be truth betrayed. He saw his opponents, Harold Joachim and William James, as tainted by some epistemological or metaphysical laxity. This can be seen in his final treatment, in *My Philosophical Development*, where he strove to associate pragmatism with nazism. His accounts of truth, varied though they were, contained nothing to justify such feelings.[13]

Iris Murdoch relied explicitly upon an explicitly metaphorical or mythological narrative. Truth, reality, and the good were brought together along the lines depicted in the *Republic*, the *Phædrus*, and the *Symposium*. Plato, she thought, "makes the assumption that value is everywhere, that the whole of life is movement on a moral scale, all knowledge is a moral quest, and the mind seeks reality and desires the good, which is a transcendent source of spiritual power, to which we are related through the idea of truth." And, again along platonic lines, the motive for the pursuit of truth was to be Eros, drawn by the magnetic force of reality.[14]

All this, to a logician, may sound as though it can be disregarded safely. Yet in a clear way it makes more consistent sense than the attitude Russell bequeathed to several generations of philosophers who followed in his tradition. Quine's treatment, in his late work entitled promisingly *Pursuit of Truth*, contained nothing on why truth should be pursued, but set off briskly: "What are true or false, it will be generally agreed, are propositions. . . ."[15] The style and substance of Russell's own occasional speculations on the pursuit of truth were wildly discordant with his other, more sober passages where he tried to pin down what truth was. For example:

> The mind which has become accustomed to the freedom and impartiality of philosophic contemplation will preserve something of the same freedom and impartiality in the world of action and emotion. It

will view its purposes and desires as parts of the whole, with the absence of insistence that results from seeing them as infinitesimal fragments in a world of which all the rest is unaffected by any one man's deeds. The impartiality which, in contemplation, is the unalloyed desire for truth, is the very same quality of mind which, in action, is justice, and in emotion is that universal love which can be given to all . . ."[16]

From this, it seems that "the unalloyed desire for truth" will stem from an appreciation of the mind's desires as "parts of the whole"—an opinion that might be understandable in view of his admiration for Spinoza, but surely at odds with his better-known attachment to atomistic pluralism. The subsequent peroration, where "through the greatness of the universe which philosophy contemplates, the mind is also rendered great, and becomes capable of that union with the universe which constitutes its highest good," is scarcely less metaphysically charged than Iris Murdoch, with far less justification.

There was an important irony in Russell's approach. Within it was implied a Humean schism between fact and value, applied to truth. We can, in varying theories, try to say what truth is, but such accounts will not tell us, at a basic level, why we want it—what its value is. Hence the embarrassingly disconnected rhetoric just quoted from the end of *The Problems of Philosophy*. If we think that we can explain, as if in factual terms, what truth is, and then leave for a preface or a peroration some account of why truth matters, then Russell's predicament may loom unavoidably. We may be left only with rhetoric. Nor could there be any escape for those, such as Quine, who like to stress the robustness of their attachment to natural facts. Truth can be instrumentally or even naturally useful, to the extent that some have sought to characterize it in just that way; but then, as Hume put it himself, "Utility is only a tendency to a certain end; and were the end totally indifferent to us, we should feel the same indifference towards the means."[17]

An account of truth which claims to be plain, neutral, or logically value-free may find that the value of truth is left unintelligibly stranded. Here is one sense in which an account of truth in terms of the truth of propositions (sentences, statements) excludes what should be most characteristic and interesting.

Iris Murdoch's resort to platonic imagery, following Plato's own highly colored accounts, was significant. Aristotle, in pragmatic contrast, opened his *Metaphysics* with the optimistic declaration that "All men by nature desire to know,"[18] which had the advantage of simplicity but the disadvantages, as a generalization, of being completely false and deeply misleading: desires for knowledge are not only not universal but are related in the most obvious ways to culturally specific values of curiosity and "natural" inquiry. Plato, on the other hand, had no wish to disentangle his form or idea of the good from knowledge and truth. It was their cause or explanation [*aitia*] in a sense he could only illuminate by his use of the image of the sun. Knowledge and truth will be "goodlike" (*agathoeidê*, a unique neologism) but not themselves good, or the good.[19]

A similar point emerges plainly, but less directly, from one contemporary rendering of truth. In Hintikka's game-theoretical semantics, truth is central both to logic and to a view of meaning: "Without the notion of truth there is little hope of capturing such basic concepts of logic as validity (truth in every model) and logical consequence." And: "a sentence means what it means by showing us what the world is like when the sentence is true. Thus the notion of truth is the be-all and end-all of sentence meaning in general." Hintikka realizes at the outset that "what a formal truth definition can do is only an abstract correlation between sentences and facts that make them true. They [*sic*] cannot provide an explanation of what it is that makes a sentence true." Here is a recognition of a potential gap between the characterization and the rôle or value of truth. It is an advantage of Hintikka's approach that such a gap is closed, as it was for Plato. But the means he used to close it were no less metaphorical than Plato's. Instead of the sun of the good illuminating the search for truth we find the imagery of games: "in my approach to meaning, truth is grounded on certain humanly playable language games." The analogy is worked out at times in productive detail:

> some degree of the mastery of the strategies of a game is unavoidable for the understanding of a game. If you only know how chessmen are moved on the board you cannot as much as say that you know how to play chess, unless you have some idea of the better and worse moves and sequences of moves. No one would deign to play chess with you. This illustrates the fact that some degree of understanding of the strategies of a game is an integral part of the conceptual mastery of that game.

Indeed so: it also helps to know that you are supposed to try to win. For Hintikka, his "original preformal game-theoretical characterization of truth" has to be in terms of "winning strategies." His view of truth, which he tells us "accords with our natural concept of truth" is "defined indirectly as the existence of a winning strategy." Games "which serve to define truth"—"semantical games"—"serve the purpose of coming to *know* the truth of the sentence in question." Evidently, he believes that the imagery of game playing offers some explanation which covers both the nature and the point of truth. The upshot, for him or for "anyone who is using a language with a minimally rich expressive power," is a "correspondence view of truth."

Our problem is the priority of any account of true sentences or propositions in an account of truth. Do we understand what is important about truth when we understand what a true sentence is? Or can we only understand what is a true sentence once we have understood truth? Hintikka believes that we need to understand the *use* of true sentences. Truth has to be a semantical relation, he thinks, but "it can exist (and perhaps must exist) only in the form of certain rule-governed activities à la Wittgensteinian language-games."[20]

One question must be how far any elucidation is achieved noncircularly. Plato created, or relied on, a rich vocabulary of vision, light, and illumination which is so entrenched in the way we talk about knowledge and truth that we can scarcely *see* how we could say anything without it: sight is the origin of philosophy. Remarkably, he saw the exact points where his imagery became indispensable and where he had to shift from *logos* to *muthos*. His use of imagery, and his steps into it, were explicit and self-conscious.[21] For Hintikka, "the interesting analogy is between the notion of truth and the existence of a winning strategy" in a game of the verification and falsification of sentences. His hope is that the circularity is only apparent, but presumably the metaphor of game playing is not meant to be optional or eliminable.[22]

A parody of old-fashioned analysis might boil down the issue impatiently to the logical relations between

(i) A understands "'p' is true"

and

(ii) A understands truth

where, for example, (i) might be a necessary condition for (ii), or (ii) might be a necessary condition for (i). This may not be as bizarre as it sounds, because very many investigations into truth have been conducted entirely in terms of the understanding of some judgment that some proposition is true. We can imagine a view that *true* can be understood only in the context of its use in statements—archetypal statements of the form of "p is true," for example—and then that one should start with the meaning of "p is true." Yet that would beg too many questions too glaringly.

≈

But if propositional truth excludes what is characteristic and interesting, what exactly is it that is excluded? Some of it can be seen in the most famous of texts on truth:

> Pilate said to him, "So you are a king?" Jesus answered, "You say that I am a king. For this I was born, and for this have I come into the world, to bear witness to the truth. Every one who is of the truth hears my voice." Pilate said to him, "What is truth?"[23]

Here we find uses of *truth* which Ramsey might have been reluctant to discuss, as "derived and metaphorical," perhaps. And we can speculate on where a line could be drawn around a nonderived and nonmetaphorical use. "I am . . . the truth," for example, from the same text,[24] must surely be a metaphor? "A witness to the truth" maybe less so? The question "What is truth?" though, might not be thought metaphorical at all. Maybe Pilate should have been more explicit and have asked, "What is a true proposition?" That sounds absurd, but the argument at this point is indeed a reductio ad absurdum. No line could be drawn except one that is chosen for our own purposes. We could, for instance, rule that the question "What is a true proposition?" is literal, factual, or suitable for logical use, where "I am the truth" is not. In effect, this has been done, historically, by many philosophers. Part of the cost might have been the misordering of what is understood, using the simplest possible test of what has been understood by very many people.

In the most banal terms, one sense of St John's condensed narrative must have been that Pilate missed the point: that truth, first of all, is valued in itself, and that this can be known before it is known how truth is to be described. The narrative does not have to be accepted, only intelligible, for this sense to emerge (and for that reason its religious tenor is irrelevant). This example must be destructive of any suggestion that a "metaphorical" (or even "religious") sense is understood because of a more direct understanding of some "literal" sense. To disagree would be to suppose that Pilate's question would have to be answered satisfactorily before the previous statement—"For this I was born . . . to bear witness to the truth"— could be understood. One assumes that this is what Pilate himself thought in the story. In platonic terms, he could not see. So his point of view would hardly be an illuminated one.

The view that some derivatively metaphorical type of truth cannot be understood unless a more central, literal type of truth is understood must be as untenable as the converse view. In fact, the prospects for any critical account of understanding, containing assertions that something *cannot* be understood *unless* something else is understood, have to be extremely bad. There are no grounds to insist that any conditions are sufficient or necessary for understanding. To root conditions for understanding in what has to be known can only be to evade this awkward fact.[25] Kant's concentration on conditions for possible knowledge, not the possible understanding of language, is not an anachronism in need of updating.

There is an analogy with Heidegger. His intimations that some older shadow of truth lurks within the sense or etymology of current use had no practical content. We can converse well enough without knowing that truth-telling was linked in ancient times to unveiling, or that truth and trust may be linked in some languages. The same applies less obviously to any assertion that the understanding of some ("literal") sense of a term must be fundamental to the understanding of some other ("derivative" or "metaphorical") sense. Such understanding may be there, or it may not. How far do we need to see the ramifications of visual metaphors to judge whether *seeing* is, or is not, metaphorical? Mary Hesse writes that "some of the mechanisms of metaphor are essential to the meaning of any descriptive language whatever." A stronger corollary would be that a contrast between the metaphorical and the literal is not only arbitrary but unsustainable.[26]

This was one great strength in Plato's use of imagery. The association in the *Republic* between the real, the good and the true was no part of a theory of meaning. Plato was neither describing a use of language nor stipulating a preferred use; nor was he arguing anything about underlying conditions. The most evident point should be that he was not arguing at all, but telling a story or showing a picture.[27] The story, in pedestrian translation, showed how truth is valuable, or is what is valued, and that it exists, or it is what exists. Presumably this is what mattered about it.

Further decoding must be risky. The kinds of questions we need to ask are exactly the ones which the form of the story repudiates. The truth is something we want; but who are *we*, and what sort of *want*? The truth relates to what exists: but how? In the *Republic* the truth was sought by philosophers, and philosophers were those who seek the truth. In the *Phædrus* the motivation was supplied or embodied by Eros. These were not explanations and cannot have been meant to be explanations; this was their merit. Surely we reach a significant dead end if we try to go further: Nietzsche's "Why not rather untruth?"[28]

WHAT IS SAID

Plato himself did not go further along these lines. He left nothing more explicit than the *Parmenides* to show his reservations about the questions posed in the works of his middle period. The *Theætetus* and the *Sophist* turned in a different direction, towards the possibility and status of false statements (among their other concerns): "The image of knowledge as direct acquaintance, as seeing with the mind's eye (although Plato does use it again later) here gives way to the conception of knowledge as use of propositions and familiarity with structure. Truth lies in discourse not in visions. . . ."[29] In his lectures on the *Sophist* of 1924–1925, Heidegger felt sure that he had located an important point of philosophical choice:

> Insofar as the Greeks ultimately developed a doctrine of *logos* in a the-
> oretical direction, they took the primary phenomenon of *logos* to be
> the proposition, the *theoretical* assertion of something about something.
> Insofar as *logos* was primarily determined on this basis, the entire sub-
> sequent logic, as it developed in the philosophy of the Occident,
> became propositional logic. . . . The understanding of . . . the usual, so-
> called systematic questions ordinarily found today in relation to logic,
> depends on a concrete investigation into the ground of the question
> of *logos* in Greek philosophy and hence here in Plato.

Much later, in *What is called thinking*, "Only because thinking is defined as *logos*, as an utterance, can the statement about contradiction perform its role as a law of thought."[30]

These interpretations may well have been too ambitious. One point, at any rate, on which Plato was unambiguous in the *Sophist* was that his *logos* was a part of what exists, not something set apart from or against it.[31] Beyond there, it hardly seems a natural conclusion that truth and falsity reside in propositions, as it were, rather than in reality. Whatever Plato's position, it was surely not an "ontologically unclarified separation of the real and the ideal" which Heidegger identified in *Being and Time* as one source of problems about truth.[32]

The point that Heidegger was trying to stress was valuable, despite its shaky textual basis. He wanted to emphasize the absence of division between an "ideal content of judgment" and a "real thing." This made him suspicious of accounts which sought to explain truth in terms of relationships between a judgment and reality, as though between two "levels" of existence. So we see a dramatized role for truth in terms of showing how things are—the pre-sentation or unveiling of reality—and an understatement of the nature of truth in terms of what is said, thought, or judged. That emphasis might be a useful corrective for those who have wanted to look at truth from the perspective of the truth of propositions.

Some uncertainty in a balance of attention between truths and reality might be understandable in terms of philosophical history; but the real difficulty stems from a lack of clear consciousness of perspective and of starting point. True propositions are supposed to tell us how things are (and false ones how they are not). How things are (or are not) may look as though it has to do with reality. Truth (and falsity) may look as though it has to do with what is said, judged or thought (about reality). In the concept of truth there seems to be some obvious link between what is said, judged, or thought and how things are (or are not). Aristotle traced one path sure-footedly: "it's not because of our truly thinking you to be pale that you are pale, but because of your being pale that we who say this have the truth."[33] This tells us that having the truth may have to do with saying *and* with what is so.

It is the order in which the link is seen that matters. If the motivating interest is in the nature of truth as seen or expressed in true statements or propositions, the appropriate question could be: what is meant by saying that it is true that you are pale? Then an appropriate answer might be that it has been said or thought that you are pale, and you *are* pale. We may feel confident about where to place *it is true that you are pale*; here we see a sample of a true proposition, the object and starting point of our interest. We may have no qualms over *you are said to be pale*; here is a sample of saying, again part of a safely identifiable context. But what about *you are pale*? Is this your paleness, literally, in the sense of a shade of your skin? Or is it the fact that you are pale? And how may it—the paleness, or the fact of the paleness—be identified or individuated except by the use of words such as "you are pale"? So maybe whatever it is has some ineradicably linguistic aspect? And so maybe no independent or autonomous existence? Along these naive lines of thinking we can start with the secure—truths—and end with uncertainty—things, states of affairs, or facts.

From a changed perspective, we could start from the existence of your paleness (Heidegger might say: its being). This may be expressed in a statement which will then be true. We may feel sure of what is so, and perhaps less sure of the determinacy or adequacy of its expression. Such a view is most familiar in a theological context. Aquinas noted that the Apostle's Creed does not say that God is almighty but "I believe in God almighty." This was not a distinction between *de dicto* and *de re* belief as much as a confidence that he could know what he could not articulate confidently. (Newman listed as one of the errors of liberalism the proposition that "No one can believe what he does not understand.")[34] It is also a perspective that should be helpful to those who have reservations about the place of truth in arithmetic.[35] Reading in one direction, from *it is true that 2 + 3 = 5*, we could say that *2 + 3 = 5* (or the proposition *that 2 + 3 = 5*) has been articulated or expressed, and 2 + 3 does = 5, although the ontological status of *2 + 3 = 5* might feel relatively more uncomfortable than the linguistic or formal status of the truth, or the true proposition. In another direction, we could start with a confidence in *2 + 3 = 5* and move towards reservations about *it is true that 2 + 3 = 5* exactly because we may feel more robust about the security of arithmetic than about the status of facts or truths.

The point here is lost in the traditionally generalized informal version—*it is true that p = it is said that p + p*—as if the use of *p* throughout can smother the difference in kind between something which is so (your skin's paleness) and a few words which happen to be in English, or an articulated thought. Christopher Williams, for example, had no problem with what he held to be a "simple" version of truth: "To say what Percy says is true is to say that things are as Percy says they are, i.e., (at least as a rough approximation) that. . . . For some *p*, both Percy says that *p* and *p*." He went on, interestingly, to argue that he saw none of the expected difficulties in *Percy says that p*: "Referential opacity is intelligible only if a wedge can be driven between substitutivity and identity, that is to say, if we can attach at least *prima facie* sense to the notion of identity without substitutivity. Here there is not even the appearance of a gap into which such a wedge could be driven."[36] This provides an ironical illustration of the asymmetry under discussion. It is indeed correct that if we start, for example, by considering *it is true that you are pale* or *what Percy says is true*, then no insuperable obstacle need be presented by *that you are pale* or by *what Percy says*. Then, *you are said to be pale* or *Percy says that p* may be treated as though, in picturesque terminology, the saying has been successfully accomplished. And, given the starting point, that is right. From an assumption that it is true that you are pale, it is reasonable enough to assume that whatever is true has been adequately identified and expressed. Dummett writes: "In so far as our aim was simply to explain the use of 'true' and 'false' as words in our language, it would therefore be entirely in order to assume, in explaining the sense of a sentence of the form 'It is true that A,' that the sentence A was itself already understood."[37] But that need not be so with the other order of reading. We can see this by running the two examples together. You are pale. Percy (a student of Aristotle) says that you are *leukos*. Is what Percy says true? In most translations, *leukos* is "white" or "fair-skinned," but it can be "pale." Percy needs to be clearer, at least, or he needs to examine his context. More generally, to start, as Williams did, from *what Percy says is true* is to assume (rightly) that Percy says something. If we begin from what is so and from Percy's attempt to express or articulate it, we should ask whether Percy has said something (or what he has said) before we can judge whether he has said something which is true. Any opacity in *what Percy says* depends on the direction from which it is viewed.

This is not quite where idealist logicians were heading in their thoughts about what they called, misleadingly, partial truth. Harold Joachim, for instance, relied on a holistic theory of sense to argue that

> No universal judgement of science . . . expresses in and by itself a determinate meaning. For every such judgement is really the abbreviated statement of a meaning which would require a whole system of knowledge for its adequate expression. . . . To take such a judgement in isolation is to take it in abstraction from the conditions under which alone its meaning can be determinate . . .

He strove to show that "Caesar crossed the Rubicon in 49BC" was not "wholly or absolutely true" because the "bare crossing of a stream," as a likely candidate for the relevant "brute fact," was an abstraction from a complicated biographical and political context.[38]

Joachim might have tried to argue that the crossing of the Rubicon by Caesar was only partly captured in the judgment that Caesar crossed the Rubicon. Seen from some other angle, the "brute fact" might have been expressed in some entirely different way. A local angler might have judged that a day's fishing on the Rubicon was being spoilt by the Roman army. A biographer might have judged that Caesar was taking a fatal step towards his downfall. A perspectivist might want to conclude that there are no brute facts, only interpretations. Joachim's thought was that the degree of truth should depend on the determinacy of meaning. A less than fully determinate judgment (as he would put it) would be less than fully true, and for him all judgments were indeterminate.

He glimpsed something helpful, but from an unhelpful direction. He should not have started from judgments at all. For him, if no judgment was made then there was nothing to be true or false. Without the articulation of a proposition, or the making of a judgment, truth or falsity could not apply. In other language, truth must depend on some form of description. Then, the "bare crossing of a stream" was no more brute or basic than "Caesar moved decisively against the republic" as a version of what happened at the Rubicon. It was another description. But we may not conclude that degrees of truth are dependent on the adequacy of descriptions. It might just as well follow that infinite possible descriptions are all true. As Joachim also intended, that line of thought would have implied great difficulties for any view of truth as correspondence. The fact, event, or state of affairs to which the proposition that Caesar crossed the Rubicon might correspond is indeed obscure. But we do not get close to any intelligible notion of partial truth.

Joachim wanted to say that no story is ever complete, so the full truth can never be told. This was upside down because unless some story is told there can be no truth. To that extent truth is dependent on a story, or language, or a judgment. Yet it must be perverse to conclude that truth resides in stories or language or judgments.[39] Following Aristotle's form of words, it is not because of our judging truly that Caesar crossed the Rubicon that he crossed the Rubicon, but because he crossed it the judgment that we make is true. The point, and the difficulty, as Aristotle surely saw, is that truth connects what is said with what is so. Yet it is far too easy to focus attention on only one side of the connection, and to see it from only one direction. In a framework of subjectivist epistemology, I can start from what I know to be the case and with how I know I talk, and end up with what I believe to be so in extra-subjective reality. In a framework which favors investigation into meanings, it will be natural to start by asking what is meant by saying that it is true that you are pale. In a nominalist framework, the investigation may end, as well as start, there. Hobbes: "*True* and *False* are attributes of Speech, not of Things. And where Speech is not, there is neither *Truth* nor *Falsehood*."[40]

An obvious objection is that we do not have to choose between what we know to be so and propositions which we hold to be true; the suggestion of some ordering of certainty is false. That may be right. Equally, it may well be right that no headway can be made in most forms of logic without an assumption that true saying is possible, leaving aside any worries about the possibility of saying. Hence the enormous reluctance to imagine any other view by those impatient to make headway in logic. Hence too the assumption made openly by Ramsey that truth could be treated in terms of what was said or judged truly. This was scarcely a matter of choice, as if he might have chosen otherwise.

Heidegger's view—or obsession—was that here was a choice that might indeed be undone, or a history that might be rewound. His forget-fulness of being (*Seinsvergessenheit*) included a forgetting of what is so in favor of what is said. His instinct that there had been some crucial point of choice was sound, though his desire to choose differently was not. A project to unravel the history of logic would be misguided as well as futile. This approach could lead to inarticulacy or mysticism: a genuine case of trying to say a good deal about what cannot be said.

What should be valuable from Heidegger, though, was an emphatic reminder that a price had to be paid for the treatment of truth in terms of the truth of what is said or judged. His insistence was that truth could be an expression or articulation of how things are: not *it is true that* . . . , but *the truth is*. . . . (An idealist understanding would be that truth should be a full expression or articulation of how things are, and that therefore normal discourse always falls short of The Truth.) The vague intimation that in aiming for truth we try to say how things are is valuable if it leads our attention to the *trying*. We can make a metaphysical drama of the point and argue that being can never be expressed fully, or that attempts at truth must always be partial, but the solid kernel within these perceptions is more modest, if more fundamental.

If the proposition that *p* is true, then there is a proposition that *p* and a proposition is something which can be true, and *p*. More neutrally, if it is *true that p*, then it is said that *p*, and *p*. We need to see the price of these conditionals. How we say what we say is held to be problematic. What we say is not. We can be sure of what is meant without being sure of how it is meant. At any rate, something along these lines must be part of the justification for the amount of attention paid to theories or accounts of meaning. There are obvious echoes from Moore's *Defence of Common Sense*:[41] we can be sure that we know without being sure how we get to know it. We may want to be confident that it is true that Caesar crossed the Rubicon while feeling less confident that we can explain how the sentence "Caesar crossed the Rubicon" has the meaning that it does.

⌣

We should reckon the costs of a choice to work with truth as the truth of what is said. The point, again, is not that we could or should make some other choice, but that a direction which has been taken has brought problems as well as gains.

The gains are obvious. It is hard to argue with the pronouncement by Frege that "Logic only becomes possible with the conviction that there is a difference between truth and untruth." He articulated the initial step in his thinking with characteristic clarity: "What is distinctive about my conception of logic is that I begin by giving pride of place to the content of the word 'true', and then immediately go on to introduce a thought as that to which the question 'Is it true?' is in principle applicable."[42] Frege's thoughts may have been succeeded as logical elements by propositions, statements, or sentences, but the significance of the step he identified has not altered. Logic is possible because truth is available in the form of true and false thoughts and their interrelationships. That is a view which can be refined endlessly, but its essential rightness must be indisputable, even for logics relying on multiple truth-values, or where the understanding of inference-rules is seen as fundamental. Ian Hacking has argued that even a thoroughgoing attempt to characterize logic as "the science of deduction," where "deducibility comes first," may still rest upon "a certain pure notion of truth and consequence," and the assumption of "classical notions of truth and logical consequence."[43]

The costs are less obvious.

Frege's own case (in "The Thought") for the indefinability of truth may have been a weak one;[44] but a wider case can be made that truth viewed essentially as the truth of a thought (proposition . . .) misses out too much of what makes truth important. As argued in this chapter, it misses out why truth matters to us—why it has a value. This matters because the severance of the description of truth from the value of truth is even more damaging than a normal severance of fact from value. Such a view was enunciated most forcefully by Nietzsche. His earlier, crude perspectivism was superseded or overlaid by a belief that the "faith in truth" or the "unconditional will to truth" was, as Maudmarie Clark sees it, "the purest form of the will to nothingness, the will directed against life, against everything that makes human life seem worth living, stripped of that which allowed it to serve life":

> you will have gathered what I am driving at, namely that it is still a *metaphysical faith* upon which our faith in science rests—that even we seekers after knowledge today, we godless antimetaphysicians still take our fire, too, from the flame lit by a faith that is thousands of years old, that Christian faith which was also the faith of Plato, that God is the truth, that truth is divine . . .[45]

Logicians may be less than keen to sign up to all of that, but at least the basis of Nietzsche's diagnosis is hard to avoid in a circular sense: if we purge the reasons why we want truth from our accounts of truth, then these accounts are not likely to tell us why truth is wanted. Accounts of truth in the form of the form of analyses of the truth of true propositions would fall into this category.

A price to be paid more within conventional logical concerns is the one which has just been discussed. If a consideration of truth is started from the truth of what is said—from the truth of true propositions—then questions about meaning will not be optional. If *it is true that p* presupposes *it is said that p* (*p* is enunciated or articulated) and this presupposes that *p is said successfully*, then it is correct that questions about meaning should precede questions about truth: we shall always need to ask how it is said that *p*, how we are able to mean what we do mean.

Again, this may look circular: if truth belongs to what is said, then saying becomes as interesting as truth. Rather, more accurately, if a decision is taken to consider truth in terms of the truth of what is said, then questions about saying will be created: how does "*p*" say that *p*? As we have seen, the pressure from such questions will depend on the direction from which they are addressed. These are real questions rooted in problems about transparency. The crux is not that they could be averted but that they are the direct consequence of a starting point in thinking about truth.

Two related issues will be pursued in the following chapters. In chapter 3 it will be argued that deadlock in the explanation of necessity stems from the treatment of what must be so in terms of what must be true. There is an obvious analogy with the view that necessity belongs first to what is said, in the form of necessary truth, not to what must be so. Chapter 5 will be a more general examination of the vague notion that we have access to how things are through language. In a naive form that is either trite or false. More sophisticated forms have their roots in assumptions that truth and necessity should be approached from what we say, that logic resides in what we say rather than how things are.

CHAPTER 3

WHAT MUST BE SO

Not everyone has found necessity problematic. Philosophers in the empiricist tradition have had the most trouble with it. We can see this as a reflection of what have been taken to be brute facts. It may be accepted that some things just exist, that some events just happen, that the world is full of contingencies, that the world of discourse is full of statements which may be either true or false. If this much is taken as unproblematic, the presence of necessity may be seen, in contrast, as needing some explanation or, perhaps, reduction. It may be less obvious that a consistent anti-empiricist might view things in reverse. For example, if everything in nature is taken to be related in an intelligible order—if it is order which is seen as a brute fact—then it may be contingency which will be unintelligible, presenting a serious problem of explanation. More weakly, if a premium is placed on some form of explicability, then necessities may be seen as comparatively well explained, and contingencies may be seen as aberrant. For example, Spinoza:

> That there are no contingent things we prove as follows:
> If something has no cause of its existence, it is impossible for it to exist.
> Something that is contingent has no cause. Therefore.
> The first [premise] is beyond all dispute. The second we prove as follows:
> If something that is contingent has a determinate and certain cause of
> its existence, then it must exist necessarily. But that something should
> be both contingent and necessary is self-contradictory. Therefore.[1]

In principle, there seems no reason why a philosopher could not be equally happy both with the contingency of things and with the unequivocal existence of necessity, and feel no desire to explain or reduce either. In practice this has not been the case.

In the classical western tradition, some philosophers have tried to portray contingency in terms of limitations on knowledge: a full understanding of the world (possibly available only to God) will reveal how it works. A genuine contrast between necessity and non-necessity may then cease to be relevant. This precipice, "which would obliterate all the beauty of the universe," was disturbing to Leibniz, who escaped its consequences only by cautious equivocation.[2] In empiricist thinking, necessities may be portrayed in terms of facts about the manipulation of ideas, about the use of language, or about decisions to treat some areas of discourse in a specially privileged way.

At this general, strategic level there cannot be much doubt that any problem in the explanation of necessity has been a problem for empiricism; in brief caricature, a type of statement (or fact) is classified as aberrant and its aberrance then creates a problem. This may suggest that philosophers have made a choice of brute facts in contrast to which other, recalcitrant facts need to be explained or reduced. In reality, things must be more complicated and therefore more interesting. Starting from some assumptions, necessity may seem to present an insurmountable challenge, to be resolved only by resort to epistemology. From other assumptions, genuine contingency may seem inexplicable or impossible. The interest lies in the imperfection of the mirror image: a kind of necessity which may be inexplicable from one starting point may not be the same as a kind which is taken for granted as unproblematic from another.

This chapter considers the general prospects for explaining necessity, with no attempt to assess specific explanatory or reductive theories such as constructivism or conventionalism. The argument is that The Problem of Necessary Truth is a problem within (or created by) a particular set of assumptions. But the conclusion is not purely abstract, only at the level of explanatory strategies; discussion of the explanation of necessity may shed light on how necessity is seen or on what it is taken to be. What necessity is, how it is to be explained, and the question of how much of a challenge it presents are all issues which are inevitably connected with each other. Such issues bear centrally on the nature of logic. Or rather, using a *tu quoque* argument, the view that they do not bear centrally on the nature of logic is questionable in itself. The view, for example, that issues about necessity belong (*only* belong) to modal logic, which has to be logically or epistemologically posterior to more basic propositional logic, contains specific assumptions that need scrutiny.

Part of the argument will be that attitudes to the explanation of necessity are intrinsic to various positions at the starting points of logic. These attitudes will include a stance of agnosticism or indifference. The view taken by Frege, for instance, that necessity was extrinsic to conceptual content (and thus, that logic could be pursued a long way without it) assumed a very specific position on necessity which created problems of its own. A view that necessity is (comparatively) uninteresting is itself an interesting view.

First, the topic in general outline; then, a particular point of choice.

NECESSARY TRUTH

Suppose, in a concern for the explanation of necessity, we start with a concern about necessary truth. This is one possible thread that can be picked up to be disentangled. Among truths, some may be false and others, it seems, may not; apparently they must be true, in some strong sense, "in all circumstances."

One way forward can be reduction: the contrast between what must be true and what may be true (or false) is only apparent. Or it may be unclear and indeterminate. What apparently must be true will be ("nothing but") what may be true or false, but perhaps with some specially entrenched status which could be changed. So there may be no fixed boundary between the necessary and the non-necessary.

There need be no difference between the explanation and the reduction of necessary truth beyond a certain hostile spirit in the case of reduction. To reduce is also to shrink. The symptomatically reductivist *nothing but* is rarely used to flatter or validate what is being explained, or explained away. Yet the reduction of necessity to non-necessity, or the denial of any workable boundary, is itself nothing but a form of explanation of necessity, and this is how it can be treated.

Starting from necessary truth, what is the problem? What needs explaining? It can only be that some truths must be true where others may not be. A problem about necessary truth has to be a problem about truth. That sounds banal. Quine packed most of the implications, as he saw them, into a few lines from 1953:

> Necessity as semantical predicate reflects a non-Aristotelian view of necessity: necessity resides in the way in which we say things, and not in the things we talk about. Necessity as statement operator is capable ... of being reconstrued in terms of necessity as a semantical predicate, but has, nevertheless, its special dangers; it makes for an excessive and idle elaboration of laws of iterated modality ...

Necessity as semantical predicate was "attachable to names of statements"; as statement operator it was attached to statements themselves.[3] As Quine said, with these necessities we are thinking of "the way in which we say things," not "the things we talk about." Implicitly, the treatment of such necessity will imply an investigation of the form of the way in which we say things, which turns out to mean logical form. In a crucial way the explanation or reduction of necessity becomes a formal explanation. And necessity attached to "statements themselves" may provoke a regress of questions: must it be true that this must be true? and so on.

Everything important is here, but it must be unpacked with care.

It has to be correct that our attention is being directed towards "the way in which we say things." If we are asking why the sentence $9 > 5$ is necessary, or even why it is necessary that $9 > 5$, then we are asking why it is necessarily true. The focus of attention is necessary truth, hence truth, and hence the truth of what is said. If anything calls for explanation or needs explaining, it has to be the special status of the truth ascribed to the sentence $9 > 5$ (in Quine's terms). An account of necessary truth, therefore, is likely to presuppose a need for some account of what it is for a sentence to be true: a theory of truth. And conversely, a comprehensive account or theory of truth may need to say something about necessary truth. Any account of the truth in true statements will have to say what it is for statements to be true (and false), and true statements may need to accommodate those which must be true, either apparently or really, depending on the approach adopted (apparently, in Quine's case).

The link between problems about necessary truth and problems about truth is not an accidental one in either direction. This must be because those who view necessity first as necessary truth will always consider necessary truths to form a narrower class than the class of truths. Necessarily true propositions (or sentences) will be seen as a subclass of true propositions, and true propositions of propositions. This background will determine the framework for explanations: the more general will be prior to the more particular. In practical terms it will also determine the order of the philosophical agenda. Where issues of truth are seen as less problematic or less controversial, some account of necessary truth may have a chance to emerge (Hume, logical positivism). When dispute rages over truth, the explanation of necessary truth may have to wait for direct discussion. As a topic, it may even seem to lose interest. For the same reason, where issues of meaning are seen as more general or fundamental than issues of truth, necessity may subside still further down the agenda.

A typical line of questions may be: What is intended by *must be true*? What is implied by *true*? What is it that is true? The point of starting creates and determines the questions which follow. These will include the questions about truth or saying which were discussed in the previous chapter. (Not always truth *and* saying, since a philosopher who regards truth as redundant will still be faced with questions about assertion, as Ramsey himself recognized.[4]) And it is striking that these will be *philosophical* questions. The point would be hard to argue decisively, given the ineradicable vagueness surrounding the nature of philosophy, but the crossing of some borderline does seem unmistakable. If we ask why the sentence $9 > 5$ is necessarily true, or why it is necessary that $9 > 5$, an explanatory or reductive answer is very likely to pass through accounts of truth or saying—meaning—which form traditional parts of philosophy, not arithmetic. This may not be accepted by anyone who feels strongly that the philosophy of mathematics is definitely part of mathematics, but it is familiar enough to librarians and to those who draw up syllabuses, or who set examinations. Arithmetical necessity turns into a philosophical problem and, *a fortiori*, an extremely intractable one.

A more definite corollary was noted by Quine: the "excessive and idle elaboration of laws of iterated modality." If an interest in necessity takes the form of attention to the special status of certain statements, for example their necessary truth, then an awkward regress beckons. In the most schematic outline: "why must it be the case that *p*?" may be answered either by "because it *is* the case that *A*," or by "because it *must be* the case that *A*" (where *A* is some explanatory theory or account). The former is overtly reductive; the latter is overtly regressive. This is too crude, because any plausible theorizing is likely to go through at least one step along the latter route: why must it be the case that *p*? because it must be the case that *A*; but why must it be the case that *A*? and then: either because it is the case that *B* or it must be the case that *B*. But the upshot is the same.[5]

NECESSITY

Suppose, in a concern for the explanation of necessity, we start with a concern about what must be so. This is one possible thread that can be picked up to be disentangled. $7 + 5$, for example, must always $= 12$. Seven mice plus five mice may amount to twelve mice, or may not, depending on how promptly they are counted.

If there is anything to be explained here, what is it? We can ask why 7 + 5 must = 12. Any explanation may refer to the rules of elementary arithmetic but need include no reference to truth. It may indeed be true that 7 + 5 = 12, but in trying to explain why 7 + 5 = 12 we do not need to say so. In teaching addition to children there is no need to mention truth; only right or wrong answers.

To explain why 7 + 5 must = 12 it may be enough to explain how 7 + 5 does = 12. In figurative terms, the necessity is not something added to a true proposition; it is an inseparable aspect of what is so. Explanation may be more or less complete or satisfactory. A reasonable, but not wholly exhaustive, explanation may be given for why, for example, 7 + 5 does or must = 12. There may be no need to cross any boundary (however vague) between arithmetic and philosophy. In asking why it must be true that 7 + 5 = 12, we ask about the truth of a statement; and so we need to know about truth and about stating—undeniably philosophical topics. In asking why 7 + 5 = 12 we ask about arithmetic, and may (or may not) be able to cite arithmetical reasons. Similarly, iterated necessities may not be generated. An explanation why 7 + 5 = 12 may be long, or even endless, generating more and more questions, but need not include any appeal to higher-level necessities.

Necessary truth can be a challenge, in large part, because it makes us ask how statements can say what they do, and how they are true. The explanation of necessity is a different business. Difficult and lengthy, perhaps, but not trailing off into the sands of the philosophy of meaning or truth.

WHAT MUST BE TRUE AND WHAT MUST BE SO

The trouble, of course, is that the contrast of perspectives seems incredible—the most elementary philosophical blunder, for a long list of reasons. A contrast between what is true and what is so will be seen as bogus and ontologically suspect. There would seem to be bad confusions between formal and material explanation, and between logical and metaphysical necessity. Some reference to *de re* and *de dicto* would seem to be missing. And the very idea of explanation without truth must seem misguided. Altogether: what a mess.

An example from arithmetic is obviously not meant to be helpful. An air of platonism hangs around a suggestion that arithmetic truths may be contrasted with what is so in arithmetic—in short, as if the statement that 7 + 5 = 12 was "about" some entities or states of affairs existing independently of it and which "made" it true—hence the ontological odium. Yet, to parody Aristotle, it is not because of our truly thinking that $7 + 5 = 12$ that $7 + 5 = 12$, but because $7 + 5 = 12$ that we who say this have the truth.[6] (Much of the underlying thinking was discussed at the end of chapter 2.) Aristotle's careful form of expression implied nothing about "independent existence." Presumably that would have amounted to an undesirable separation (*chôrismos*) of the Forms, in his terms. It is not the existence of some entities, 7, +, 5 and so on, which makes $7 + 5 = 12$ true. It is just because $7 + 5 = 12$. Trivially, it is not possible to say that it is true that $7 + 5 = 12$ without saying (somehow) that $7 + 5 = 12$, but that truism could hardly be the basis for some nominalistic conclusion that it is ("only") because of our truly saying that $7 + 5 = 12$ that $7 + 5 = 12$ (or the basis for a realistic denial of such a conclusion).

Second, there may well seem to be a bad confusion between formal and material explanation. In the one case, we try to explain why it is necessarily true that $7 + 5 = 12$, with the repercussions we have seen. In the other, we explain why or how $7 + 5 = 12$. Here, surely, is some failure to distinguish an examination of the syntax of modal propositions from an inquiry into the grounds for modalities: logical from metaphysical necessity? But the whole point is that if we do begin, in Quine's words, with "the way in which we say things," then it will be the way in which we say things which will be the focus of our investigation: the logical form of what we say. If we begin differently, then we are faced with different challenges, but not challenges of syntax, semantics, or logical form. Many of the problems of interpretation surrounding Hume's treatments of necessity derive from a blurring of perspectives: a slide between a discussion of what might be interesting initially—why and how far something had to happen—and a discussion of why certain propositions might be held to be necessarily true. The fact that I may be able to imagine the falsity of certain propositions about the movement of billiard balls should have no bearing on why billiard balls move as they do.

Similarly, a contrast between *de re* and *de dicto* should be out of place. If a *de re* form is seen as *it is true that necessarily A* in contrast with a *de dicto, it is necessarily true that A*, then that contrast is out of focus in two connected ways. The contrast we are now considering is one between what must be true—the necessary truth of what is said—and what must be so—how things must be. That is not a contrast between two types of truth whose logical forms we may then compare. The *explicanda* are of different kinds. It may be of interest to ask why *it is true that necessarily A*, but that is not the same as to ask why A must be so. We are not aiming to get within one form of saying into another one—Quine's third grade of modal involvement—but to ask questions which have little to do with saying.

Far more seriously, explanation without truth may look implausible. Even if it is allowed that problems in the explanation of what must be true are of a different order and severity from problems in the explanation of what must be so, the latter type of explanation may seem to suggest enough difficulties of its own. How, for example, could anything explain, even incompletely, that 7 + 5 must = 12 without bringing in basic logical relationships of entailment, implication, or consistency which could only hold between basic logical building blocks such as judgments, sentences, statements or propositions? In aiming to say "7 + 5 must = 12 because . . . ," are we not expecting to explain why one proposition must be true by showing how others are true? And thus failing to escape problems about truth and meaning after all?

This begs the question in a revealing way by taking for granted that an explanation has to stand in some logical relation to its *explicandum*, where a logical relation is assumed to be some relation between the truth or falsity of propositions. It is further taken for granted that logical relations must be more readily intelligible than explanations, which is at least questionable. There is a parallel with the contrast, frequently underlined in the work of Donald Davidson, between "the analysis of causality" and the "logical form of causal statements." Davidson has remarked that "it is sentences (or statements or propositions), or the relations between them, that are properly classified as contingent or logical; if causal relations are 'in nature,' it makes no sense to classify them as logical or contingent."[7] What he said about causality applies by analogy to explanation. In the case of causal explanation it applies exactly.

LEIBNIZ

These skeletal arguments about the explanation of necessity and necessary truth are dead without real philosophical flesh on their bones. In the abstract, it may not seem so controversial, for example, that a logical version of necessity engenders logical problems. But why should this matter? After all, it is not as if we are presented with some choice of necessities now and need to decide on one form to adopt. Rather, the point is that there was a divergence in the past, but not a complete one. It seemed easier, for sensible reasons, to deal with necessary truth—with logical necessity. But that led to strains in carrying the weight it had to bear. It may be unworkable to go back and take a different route, though we can try to reckon the cost of the one that was taken.

It was taken, not for the first time, but most famously, by Leibniz. The clearest step can be seen in his paper "On Freedom." It opened with a dubious understatement:

> One of the oldest doubts of mankind concerns the question of how freedom and contingency are compatible with the chain of causes and providence. And Christian investigations of the justice of God in accomplishing man's salvation have merely increased the difficulty of the matter.

This was less than frank. In fact, almost all the difficulty came from religion, as is suggested by the strangely ambivalent "chain of causes and providence." If there were no problems about providence and divine choice, the simplest imaginable solution would have been to hand. In plain terms, everything is determined, but our inadequate minds do not give us enough information about what is due to happen. Leibniz's problem was that his God had to possess not just a noninadequate mind but an infinite mind, and also some awkward moral qualities such as justice and benevolence—one aspect of a larger problem, of how to reconcile new natural philosophy with the requirements of traditional theology. Here, in particular, what worried him was "possible things which neither are nor will be nor have been," for "if certain possible things never exist, existing things cannot always be necessary; otherwise it would be impossible for other things to exist in their place, and whatever never exists would therefore be impossible." It is the step taken away from this deadlock which is of interest. "Having . . . recognized the contingency of things," he wrote, "I raised the further question of a clear concept of truth, for I had a reasonable hope of throwing some light from this upon the problem of distinguishing necessary from contingent truths." His concern was about what has to happen, God's freedom of choice, and what had to exist. His route to a solution required an immediate discussion of truths and a dive into his theories about the infinite analysis of propositions. A shift from the contingency of things to contingent truths let him handle logical rather than metaphysical modalities. Characteristically, a metaphysical problem slid towards a logical solution.[8] To solve problems about necessity he produced an explanation for necessary truth. The step was a smooth one. Leibniz wrote of a "wonderful secret . . . which contains the nature of contingency or the essential distinction between necessary and contingent truths and which removes the difficulty involved in a fatal necessity determining even free things." The secret was that "first truths" were to be "those which predicate something of itself or deny the opposite of its opposite" and that "all other truths are reduced to first truths with the aid of definitions or by the analysis of concepts."[9] But neither this nor his distinction between absolute and hypothetical necessities touched the root of his real difficulty. Leibniz wanted to ground his view that, for example, "the individual concept of each person includes once and for all everything which can ever happen to him" in his doctrine of the inclusion of the predicate in the logical subject. The awkward step from language (or logic) to "everything which could ever happen" was bridged by an uncomfortably wide use of *concept*. "Everything that happens to some person is already contained virtually in his nature or concept" [est déjà compris virtuellement dans sa nature ou notion] does not tell us whether the concept was nearer to the person or to some thought about the person. If the latter, then the theory would be in danger of melting down into a truism that a full description of a person will contain "everything." The former might or might not be correct, but this is what Leibniz had to demonstrate, not something he could assume. What he wanted to say was that "every true predication has some basis in the nature of things," but the vagueness of "some basis" was hardly helpful.[10] It was because a logical predicate was contained in its subject that a substance contained its properties. Leibniz believed that "physical necessity" was "derived from metaphysical necessity," and not the reverse. (With metaphysical necessity, a contrary "would imply a contradiction or logical absurdity.")[11]

His explanatory approach generated great problems. He thought that his notion of the analysis of a logical subject, with the allied notion of inclusion, was a useful one which could at least shed light on the analysis of the concept of a substance. The metaphor of analysis acquires all its force from its physical sense: we cut something up into its parts. Yet it was the analysis of the logical subject which was supposed to shed light on the analysis of a substance or its concept. Which explained or illuminated which? Even if there was a noncircular explanation for metaphysical or logical necessities— for necessary truths—the connection with the necessities that Leibniz really needed to explain was left undetermined. The useful ambivalence between the analysis of a substance (or the concept of an individual substance) and of a logical term continued at least until it reached its reductio ad absurdum in Russell's *Philosophy of Logical Atomism*:

The reason that I call my doctrine *logical* atomism is because the atoms I wish to arrive at as the sort of last residue in analysis are logical atoms and not physical atoms. Some of them will be what I call "particulars"—such things as little patches of color or sounds, momentary things—and some of them will be predicates or relations and so on. The point is that the atom I wish to arrive at is the atom of logical analysis, not the atom of physical analysis[12]

It is a tribute to the persuasiveness of the imagery that even eighty years after this was written there may be many who still do not see its absurdity.

A natural thought is that the connection between concepts and nature should have been made through truth. Robert Merrihew Adams wrote that Leibniz's distinction between necessity and contingency "is based on a difference in the logical form of the reasons by virtue of which propositions of the two sorts are true."[13] Again, "every true predication has some basis in the nature of things." So if we explain the necessity of a necessarily true proposition, the fact of its truth will mean that we may also explain how things must be as they are. If that is right, it is in line with one assumption in this chapter: a theory of truth is required to deal with necessary truth. There is no need to pursue the details of Leibniz's explanations. He was led towards the luxuriance of possible worlds where necessary truths could be true. Again, it is worth asking what might be expected to explain what. In more modern terms, the truth of necessary truths might be thought to be intelligible in nonactual possible worlds through some form of modelling. Then there might or might not be some question about the ontological propriety of those worlds, depending on the robustness of the theorist at work. That was not Leibniz's approach at all. He started with his preconceptions of what was and was not really necessary ("in the world")—preconceptions determined by religious requirements—and then turned to necessary and contingent truths as a way to shed light on what must be so. (A reversal of Russell's understanding that "Leibniz's philosophy was almost entirely derived from his logic."[14]) If we feel generous, we can say that there could have been a self-reinforcing circularity between the assured existence of God and the guaranteed truth of necessary truths: "it is necessary for eternal truths to have their existence in an absolutely or metaphysically necessary subject, that is, in God, through whom those possibilities which would otherwise be imaginary are (to use an outlandish but expressive word) realized."[15] Without such confidence in God's existence, "eternal truths" would be left hanging nowhere as the derivation for "physical necessity."

SPINOZA

In 1676 Leibniz met Spinoza. He claimed to be appalled by his views, particularly on necessity and divine choice. Spinoza was uninterested in logic, which he regarded as a sort of mental hygiene. His use of logical terms was exasperatingly informal, even by seventeenth-century standards. (Leibniz complained in a note on the *Ethics*, for example, that no definition of contingency was given. His mistake was understandable because he would hardly expect to find a term defined in Part IV of a work after it had been used copiously in Part I.[16]) Spinoza's understanding of necessity was concrete: "That thing is said to be free which exists solely from the necessity of its own nature, and is determined to act by itself alone. A thing is said to be necessary or rather, constrained, if it is determined by another thing to exist and act in a definite and determinate way."[17] Two points about this definition are obvious immediately. Things were necessary, not propositions. Their necessity consisted in having determining causes. It followed that there could be no problem in the explanation of necessity. On the contrary, put bluntly, if something was necessary it had an explanation—a cause or reason. Interestingly, Leibniz made no comment on this definition in his notes on the *Ethics*, although he had plenty to say about its consequences.

The challenge for Spinoza, as for Leibniz, was with contingency, not necessity. Their responses looked similar but were radically different. For Leibniz, the secret of contingency lay in the infinite analysis of contingently true propositions: "only God being able to see, not the end of the analysis indeed, since there is no end, but the nexus of terms or the inclusion of the predicate in the subject, since he sees everything which is in the series."[18] The infinite analysis of a subject moves straightaway into an area of unintelligibility not uncongenial to Leibniz's sense of piety. His use of infinity was hyperbolic. His point would have been as well made if he had said that the analysis of contingently true propositions was too difficult for (current) human understanding and that God understands things better; but he wanted a tidy polarity between finite-human and infinite-divine.

Spinoza's approach to the understanding of necessity differed in at least three ways from Leibniz's. First, he thought primarily in terms of causes of things, not the truth of propositions. Individuals ("in nature") were interconnected in an infinite causal net. And "because the chain of causes [*ordo causarum*] is hidden from us, then the thing cannot appear to us as either necessary or as impossible. So we term it either 'contingent' or 'possible'." So contingency was related to a "deficiency in our knowledge." In reality, "nothing in nature is contingent."[19] The notion of an endless causal net, while not being without problems, remains far more transparent than Leibniz's infinite analyses of logical subjects. Secondly, Spinoza's God was not an external spectator or chooser. Endless chains of causes (mental or corporeal) existed "in" God, but this cannot be read in the sense that God was thinking about them, or could be thinking about them in any remotely anthropomorphic sense. Thirdly, Spinoza had no interest in explaining the sense of what might be said or thought. His approach to modality was concerned with existence, not with the meaning or truth of statements of possibility or necessity. The fact that we can formulate counterfactual possibilities, for example, did not impress him. Again, "Many more ideas can be constructed from words or images than from merely the principles and axioms on which our entire natural knowledge is based."[20] We can say things that are not correct. This was not interesting.

The corollaries from Spinoza's approach seem paradoxical. He started the *Ethics* with his God, and yet it turns out that his account of necessity was markedly less theological, both in its impetus and in its consequences, than Leibniz's. The extreme immanence of his thinking meant that necessity, for example, could only exist within nature. His God was literally in no position to guarantee or underwrite truths. So there was no room for iterations of necessity and still less for possible worlds; the reason why something was necessary would have been the cause or reason why it was as it was, which would have been a "natural" explanation, and beyond nature was nothing. Ironically, too, the allegedly archrationalist Spinoza ended up with some highly unrationalistic-looking attitudes. In the *Theological-Political Treatise* he concluded that "for practical purposes it is better, indeed, it is essential, to consider things as contingent" because "we plainly have no knowledge as to the actual co-ordination and interconnection of things—that is, the way in which things are in actual fact ordered and connected."[21] Although he was more ready to face the consequences of determinism than Leibniz, the pragmatic outcome of his position was not far from Hume: "when we have regard only to the essence of Modes and not to the order of Nature as a whole, we cannot deduce from their present existence that they will or will not exist in the future or that they did or did not exist in the past."[22]

The evident obstacle seems to be that the type of necessity used by Spinoza was not the type of necessary truth discussed by Leibniz. That is right but again ironic, because it was a set of problems about divine necessitation which initiated Leibniz's thinking. He did not start off trying to characterize the necessity of necessarily true propositions: he moved to this from substantive questions about God's freedom of choice and human capacities for salvation. The issue he left open was whether his solutions to questions about logical necessity could be applied back into the contexts from which they originated. It is surprising that this has not been seen more often as strange. He launched into his treatment of necessary truths to resolve concerns about what must be so, but ended up by bequeathing concerns about the relationship between necessary truths and reality. We might suspect a needless detour.

Spinoza never shifted into a treatment of necessary propositions, and so his discussions of why things must be as they are were entirely concrete. This meant that everything depended for him on necessitation, which came down to the fact of possessing a *ratio, seu causa*: "the reason or cause why God, or nature, acts, and the reason or cause why he exists, are one and the same."[23] The upshot was that the reason or cause became a fundamental relationship, replacing not only logical connectives but also the ties of natural law. Spinoza is often assumed to have absorbed causality into a logical relationship such as entailment. It would be truer to say that he treated logical relationships as less basic or as less intelligible than causality.[24] The passage just quoted from the *Theological-Political Treatise* was preceded by a methodological maxim—"We ought to define and explain things through their proximate causes. Generalizations about fate and the interconnection of causes can be of no service to us in forming and ordering our thoughts concerning particular things . . ."—and followed by the dry comment: ". . . So much for law taken in the absolute sense." Which takes us back to Davidson: "if causal relations are 'in nature,' it makes no sense to classify them as logical or contingent."[25]

LEIBNIZ OR SPINOZA?

But if these two conceptions of necessity were so different, why should they be compared, and why should there be any thought of choice between them? Or rather, why should there be any point in thinking about choice now, since there certainly were real alternatives at the end of the seventeenth century? Spinoza's approach seems a historical curiosity, while Leibniz's—in strategic outline, not in detail, minus God—became standard. An implied problem about the relationship between truths and reality became an openly epistemological problem: how are the judgments that I make possible? The nature and explanation of necessity became tied to the "possibility" of necessary truths in a specific epistemological context. From Kant onwards, the problem became how to account for a form of judgments, then propositions: "Experience teaches us, to be sure, that something is constituted thus and so, but not that it could not be otherwise. First, then, if a proposition is thought along with its necessity, it is an *a priori* judgment. . . ."[26] During the long reign of subjectivist epistemology, issues about the form and status of necessities were just another set of questions about how I can know—or seem to know—what I think I know about ("external") reality. Later still, it became natural to worry only about the form of judgments or statements, forgetting or even repudiating the context in which this had made some sense.

Once again, there would be no point in suggesting that this history should or could be unthreaded, as if a wrong path had been taken and we need to retrace our steps. Nor are there any sensible terms in which we can imagine that Leibniz was wrong and Spinoza was right. They were both faced with similar concerns created by the grandiose pretensions of the new physics. Already by 1647, Descartes had been confident enough to assert that he had in his grasp "all the principles which I use to deduce the truth of other things." These, he thought, were "principles which enable us to deduce the knowledge of all the other things to be found in the world" (although admittedly "many centuries may pass before all the truths that can be deduced from these principles are actually so deduced").[27] Total explanation seemed within reach.

We can speculate whether the root of the difference in approach between Leibniz and Spinoza was religious. Leibniz wanted to achieve consistency with the needs of Christian theology, in pursuit of characteristically seventeenth-century preoccupations with salvation, divine grace, and free will. Spinoza certainly did not. His reading of the *Epistle to the Romans* was that divine law—both moral and natural, equally—was not to be seen as "prescribed" but, for human beings, as "inscribed deep in their hearts" and, for the rest of nature, as part of it, not separate. He wrote in a letter, none too grammatically, of "laws, or nature."[28]

For Spinoza there seems to have been no doubt that the basis for his form of necessity was in the things we talk about, and not in the way in which we talk about things. That, too, left large questions of epistemology, but in a different direction. He never accepted the cartesian construction of radical doubt. He thought that people, as part of nature, had a less or more competent grasp of nature, including themselves. They might express that grasp less or more competently, but their forms of expression would reveal nothing about how nature is or must be. From the cartesian standpoint adopted by Leibniz, perception of the contents of my mind and my account of those contents in a language was not a problem. For Spinoza, such understanding and its expression was a prime source of error: "Most controversies arise from this, that men do not correctly express what is in their mind." But how nature is (geometrically, for example) was something we can find out. There was no question of how such knowledge could be possible, as if it might not be possible; though we could ask how what had to be so, was so. Science was not only possible but adequately supported and thus, in Spinoza's sense, necessary.[29]

Leibniz's angle was successful and productive. A metaphor of nature governed by laws led to immense amounts of science. Scientists themselves paid little attention to the awkward points in the metaphor: the logical status of laws and their relationship to the world they governed. In practical terms these did not matter.

In the longer run, one of the great problems in necessary truth came from its unrevisable hardness. As we have seen, explanations of necessary truth have a tendency towards iteration. This can be taken negatively or positively. Negatively, a reductive theorist may wish to undermine any notion of necessity. It may be argued that no necessary truth can ever be formulated in a way in which it is itself necessarily true. In a simple linguistic reduction of necessity, for example, nothing about language use can ever be completely unrevisable in the last resort. So no explanation could be strong enough. Or positively, a very strong claim that necessary truth has to be true in all possible worlds can be a severe embarrassment when alleged necessities turn out to be subverted by later discoveries. The suspicion is sown that any presumed necessity may be liable to subversion. This was to be the fate of Kant's synthetic a priori principles. Everyone wants necessity to be a hard notion, but it should not be so hard that it loses credibility and cracks as soon as strains are applied. Much of the critique in "Two Dogmas of Empiricism" used this strategy.[30] The demands of necessary truth were too high ever to be fulfilled; so necessity was a flawed notion.

Paradoxically, given Spinoza's reputation for dogmatism, his approach allowed more flexibility. Spinoza himself would not have been impressed by the idea of better- or worse-entrenched necessities. He thought in the absolutist terms of a single, coherent system. The reasons why anything had to be so would be the *ratio, seu causa* why it was so. Such reasons might be found to alter or weaken. His view could have allowed for less or more thorough explanations, without a false turning towards Leibnizian relative necessities.

It is intriguing that he took a more cautious line on arithmetic than on geometry. His reasons were weird but strangely prescient: numbers depend on the imagination, geometry on the pure conception of extension.[31] This remains relevant because Gödel's results might seem to have been the decisive end for spinozistic holism. There must be truths in arithmetic for which no comprehensive *ratio, seu causa* can be given. Spinoza must have felt that $7 + 5 = 12$ had a less secure basis than the theorems of euclidean geometry. Straying a long way into anachronism, we hold now that there may be provable results in geometries where questions of truth seem pointless. Spinoza's approach would have allowed truth and necessity (or proof) to be prised apart, as they were in the later history of mathematics. A view of necessity as necessary truth makes that impossible.

CONTENT

For Spinoza, to explain why something was necessary was to explain why it was so. Thus, there was no special problem of necessity, though there could be formidable problems in explaining why things were as they were (that would be natural philosophy). For Leibniz, necessity was approached as necessary truth. The question became why some propositions had to be true. The problem was one of finding reasons for the status of necessarily true propositions (for him that was theology; for his successors it would be philosophy or logic). Necessity had been externalized.

We see a similar move in Kant, who wrote that modality "contributes nothing to the content of the judgment (for besides quantity, quality, and relation, there is nothing more that constitutes the content of a judgment) but rather concerns only the value of the copula in relation to thinking in general." He had in mind an epistemological distinction, later expressed explicitly in the *Jäsche Logic*: "Truth is an *objective property* of cognition; the judgment through which something is *represented* as true, the relation to an understanding and thus to a particular subject, is, *subjectively, holding-to-be-true.*"[32] Maybe through the influence of Lotze, Frege followed a related line: "If I call a proposition necessary, I thereby give a hint as to my grounds for judgment. *But since this does not affect the conceptual content of the judgment, the apodeictic form of a judgment has no significance for us.*"[33] Because the necessity of a proposition was held to be external to its conceptual content, in its "grounds," Frege felt entitled to sidestep discussion on necessity until questions more immediate for him had been resolved.

At the same time, a sharply different approach was being taken by F. H. Bradley (who was even more severe than Frege on psychologism in logic— he liked to call Mill, with a heavy sneer, "our great modern logician"):

> Modality may be supposed to affect the assertion in its formal character, and without regard to that which is asserted. We may take for instance a content S-P, not yet asserted, and may claim for modality the power of affirming this content S-P, unaltered and unqualified, in several ways. S-P, it is supposed, may be asserted, for instance, either simply or problematically or apodeiktically, and may yet remain throughout S-P: and thus, though the content is unmodified, the assertion is modal.

Bradley's arguments against this "erroneous view" were confused. If a judged content is affirmed, then "it is declared to be a fact, and it cannot be more or less of a fact." On the basis of his idealism he could argue that a proposition judged in one way is never the same as when it is judged in another way. But he could have filled out a much more convincing case. The suggestion that the same judgment—or the contents of the same judgment—asserted on different grounds, might have differing modal values, was deeply implausible, raising the most serious problems about identity (or, taking a different line, a meltdown in the notion of identifiable propositions). Even in propositional terms, it seems reasonable to say that if a necessary proposition is understood, then its truth must be understood. So there could be no way in which a proposition could be held to be necessary (on some grounds) and not necessary (on others). In an uncontroversial, non-Bradleian sense, that could not be the same proposition. But in fact, Bradley's view of necessity was not in any way propositional:

> A thing is necessary if it is taken not simply in and by itself, but by virtue of something else and because of something else. Necessity carries with it the idea of mediation, of dependency, of inadequacy to maintain an isolated position and to stand and act alone and self-supported. A thing is not necessary when it simply *is*; it is necessary when it is, or is said to be, *because of* something else.[34]

And in these nonpropositional terms, the point could be still clearer. If a "thing" was understood, then its necessity would be understood. It could not be understood as not necessary, or it would not be what it was.

Frege's hope that necessity might be external to (and thus detachable from) propositional content was an outcome of the choice of approach made by Leibniz. In one way it made modality manageable, in a sense of formal manipulation, but in another it was a reductio ad absurdum of an unsustainable position. The quotation above, from *Begriffsschrift*, for example, looks like wishful thinking. The "conceptual content" in the assertion of a necessary proposition, for example, might be thought to tell us everything about the strength of its "grounds," not merely to hint at them.

A general rule was enunciated in the *Grundlagen*: ". . . the question as to how we arrive at the content of a judgment has to be distinguished from the question as to how we provide the justification for our assertion." Frege's support for this wide claim was surprisingly feeble: "It frequently happens that we first discover the content of a proposition and then provide a rigorous proof in another, more difficult way, by means of which its validity can often also be discerned more precisely. Thus. . . ."[35] He wanted to say that "how we arrive at the content of a judgment" was independent of "how we provide the justification for our assertion." In mathematical terms, what he meant was obvious. Yet his argument cut both ways. In one direction he could discover a content first and then give a proof: the two steps, by implication, were a symptom of two separable stages (a specimen of the cartesian argument discussed in chapter 1). But in the other direction, a proof could allow the validity of a proposition to be "discerned more precisely." Understanding of content could precede (and hence be separate from) understanding of proof-grounds; yet the understanding of a proof could affect the understanding of content: what else was meant by "more precisely"? This can look like common sense, with a common-sense escape from the obvious objection; we grasp content partly, but then an understanding of a proof may improve or complete that grasp. But difficulties then arise both in theory and in application. In theory, the distinction between content and ground becomes blurred to the extent that the required conceptual separation can no longer be achieved. In practice, we might wonder what could be meant by grasping the judgeable content of the proposition that $7 + 5 = 12$ without grasping—or separately from grasping—that $7 + 5$ must $= 12$. The association between grounds and proof was destined for trouble.

Frege illustrates how an attitude towards the explanation of necessity can be linked to a specific view on the position of necessity. This is striking because his overt attitude towards the explanation of necessity was one of comparative indifference: the subject did not greatly occupy him. Although his position can be seen well enough, he did not work it out himself with the attention that he gave to most of his work. Questions about why arithmetical propositions were necessarily true might be important, but they could be placed outside questions about the content and truth of arithmetical propositions.

Some later philosophers have been inclined to blur or close the separation between content and grounds for necessities, but the cost can be high. Some have claimed that modality is determined by the structure or form of what is said: that ground and content are interdependent. Others have claimed that pure content is an illusion, and that modality depends only on how we say what we do say. But if necessity is to be sited in what is said (or thought or judged), the question becomes why some of what is said has to be true. Then, the alternatives that present themselves are that some things which are said must be true either in virtue of their logical or linguistic structure—something internal to them—or in virtue of something external to them—the way they are held, known, or treated (or some mixture of both). Frege himself went for the latter alternative in theory— for external grounds—although his views (for most of his life) on the analyticity of arithmetic also left a trail towards the other direction.

∾

This has been a case study in choice before logic, not just before modal logics.

It was no accident that Spinoza was uninterested in logic. His understanding of the necessitation of things would have been hard to develop into any kind of logical system, even one with extremely intensional and *de re* foundations. So we cannot go back to him to dig out the roots of a different possible history. Leibniz's approach, through the necessary truth of propositions, had the eventual effect of distilling modality from content, making possible the development of both logics and modal logics. We have seen some of the cost in the legacy of problems of explanation or intelligibility. It is not too trite to say that necessity ceased to be what was explainable only to become what had to be nonexplainable.

The choice of approach made by Leibniz was by no means distinct, and this may give an impression that no decisive move had been made. Actually, it was the lack of distinctness—the failure to make a clean break with the past—which is important. We have not seen two distinct versions of necessity: one explicable by definition but problematic in its value to logic, and another leading to modern logics but leaving a residue of problems about explanation. Rather, Leibniz's choice was a muddled one. He wanted to deal with real questions about divine freedom and foreknowledge by translating them from metaphysics into questions about the necessary truth of propositions. His own answers continued to rely on theological assumptions (in modern terms) to underwrite the semantics for his logic. Later writers have hoped to wash out the taint of theology. Yet Leibniz's approach contained a circle of explanation that was not easy to remove. Physical necessity was to be explicable in terms of metaphysical necessity (and this was only another way of saying that metaphysics was to be turned into logic), but metaphysical modality was itself made intelligible through physical metaphors. More tellingly, Leibniz wanted to read back into nature the consequences of his propositional understanding of modality. This embroiled him in a deep ambivalence towards determinism. More widely, there was a far worse problem. If what must be so is translated into what must be true, then we can always ask whether (or how) anything that happens has to happen or whether anything that exists has to exist. If the answer is rigorously no, then we are left with the view that things and events in nature may be less or more explained, depending on the state of our knowledge, which was fundamentally the view of Spinoza. If the answer is yes, then we need to go back to nature to find out what is necessary and what is not, which negates the gain from the move into logic. Kant's synthetic a priori only made this dilemma more painful, by locating necessity outside our judgments and by making nature in itself wholly inaccessible.

The argument in chapter 1 was that a version of possibility was dependent on absolutist assumptions that had undeniably theological origins. There is some parallel with necessity. Heidegger wrote that the contention that there are "eternal truths" belonged "to the remnants of Christian theology" within a philosophical problematic that had not yet been radically eliminated.[36] Certainly, Leibniz relied on theological hyperbole. Without the eternal and infinite mind of God he would have had nowhere to put his modalities. We may want to believe that his approach can be modernized untheologically, looking elsewhere for a source of logical compulsion and hoping for a notion of law without a lawgiver. Curiously, Spinoza, who was quite untroubled by the requirements of Christian theology, was there before us.

CHAPTER 4

TALKING ABOUT THINGS

This book offers illustrations of choices "before logic." Some of the general implications were spelt out in the Introduction. There need be no discussion of whether we have a choice of logics. At least with an understanding of logics as formal systems, that is not debatable. Nor need we spend time on any alleged bases or foundations of logic, or logics. Again, where differing forms of logic are accepted, the existence of different fundamentals (or in some cases, the denial of any) will be evident.

Charles Taylor's description of "pre-logical mentality" as an absurdity might be justifiable in a context of historical social anthropology.[1] Here, rather, there would be some absurdity in demanding clear logic before logic. The aim is to look at some unclear thinking which is not a formal foundation for any sort of logic, but which can suggest starting points from which different expectations for logic can arise. So far as there are any questions of priority, they can only be about the *Metaphysical Foundations of Logic* against *The Logical Basis of Metaphysics*,[2] but the opposition is not genuine. There is a two-way relationship between "philosophical" assumptions and "logical" choices which should be corrosive of foundationalism in either direction. There may be different ways of looking at things which suggest different routes in logic, which in turn suggest different ways of looking at things. That may sound banal. The interest starts when we expect our logic to work in a context where it is not at home.

PROPERTIES AND INGREDIENTS

Accounts of things may be given in different ways. The features given within any account may be unlimited in number. The different forms of account of a thing may be unlimited in number. These uncontentious facts mean that the notion of a complete or final account is illusory: there may always be more to say. We may pick out two apparently different forms of account of a thing (among others): the first in terms of its ingredients, parts, elements, or constitution; the second in terms of its properties (including relational ones) or qualities. A fruitcake is made of flour, sugar, eggs, fruit, and so on. It has the properties of being cylindrical, having a certain weight and texture, looking brown, tasting fruity, and so on. A particular fruitcake may have particular ingredients and may have particular properties, including the relational properties of being in a particular position at a particular time and so on. On a more interesting level, a neutron is made up of one up quark and two down quarks and has the property of having no charge.

Interests in the ingredients or in the properties of things can lead inquiries into divergent directions. An interest in ingredients seems—or seemed for a long time in the history of science—to lead to a dead end, both physically and metaphysically. Until very recently, nothing could be said competently about ultimate physical ingredients. Metaphysically, whenever the pitfalls of atomism have been understood, they have discouraged philosophers from making assertions about ultimate constituents. An interest in properties, on the other hand, seems to have been less insecurely founded and to have had much greater utility. In physical terms it provided the justification for endless observation, especially when properties were identified wholly or partly with perceptual qualities. Philosophically, it can lead on to asking which properties of things matter more than others and hence to the formulation of determinate descriptions—definitions—in terms of those which matter most of all. This in turn can lead to the study of relations between such descriptions and so to logic and to much useful science.

The early stages in this possible divergence of interest cause no real problems. In one sense, simple descriptions of things in terms of their ingredients or their properties need not differ in any interesting way. But difficulties set in around the modal notions of necessity and essence. The argument here will be that essences can be related more readily to accounts of things in terms of their ingredients than to accounts in terms of properties. Conversely, attempts to portray essences in terms of essential properties can become problematic. Much of the interest lies in the very lack of clarity of the point. One entirely worthwhile approach can be to show that the purported arguments in support of a philosophical theory are defective.[3] Another may be to show how theories can have confused or even contradictory origins: historical origins, but also origins through the ways in which we start thinking or talking about things.

The notion of alternative forms of account is central. That we (today, in English) are able to describe some objects in terms of their properties and in terms of their ingredients can scarcely be doubted. The philosophical interest gets going when this point is pressed. Is there, for example, a basic or fundamental form of description to which others can be reduced or assimilated? If there is, does this suggest a basic or fundamental form of logic related to it in some way? If there is not, does that mean there are distinct, nonreducible forms of description? If we can think in terms of only one basic form of description, then the notion of a distinct form of description seems illusory (in that there would be no countable alternatives). If we cannot, then we seem to be heading for relativism or perspectivism. The arguments at this point seem to mirror those surrounding the viability of alternative discourses, conceptual schemes, or narratives.

The relation between presumed forms of description and forms of logic may seem tenuous. There seems to be a nice analogy between property-based description and predicative logic on the one hand and ingredient-based description and mereology on the other. It looks as if this analogy might be given some historical substance. In the case of Aristotle, for example, there seems to be a plausible link between subject-predicate logic, object-property metaphysics, and a corresponding rejection of definition in terms of parts or ingredients. In the case of Frege, there seems to be a plausible link between functional logic, object-concept metaphysics, and a rejection of a logic "in which the fundamental relation is that of part to whole."[4] Yet the plausible link in Aristotle by no means coincides with the plausible link in Frege. And the connection between loose forms of description—or metaphysical views—and forms of logic is hard to sustain in both cases.

Yet the whole point is missed if we go for decisive formal clarity. Formally, it can be argued that mereological logics are reducible to predicate logics without too much dispute. With rather more dispute, the reverse reduction might be argued. It is possible, but not uncontroversial, to argue the closest association between logical predicates and ("metaphysical") properties. Modality can be attached either to predicate logics or to mereologies. So, it might seem, discussions about priority are a waste of time.

All this is reasonable but beside the point. It must be correct that an attempt at a basic or fundamental form of description is mistaken. Some forms of description can be reduced to each other with varying degrees of plausibility. But there is only an indistinct, loose relationship between forms of description and forms of logic. Philosophical difficulties can occur—can be induced—where there is insistence on too much simplicity, clarity, or exclusivity. We can try to banish relativism by insisting that one form of description is fundamental, or we can welcome it by insisting that irreducible forms of description are available. But in reality, forms of description overlap and intermingle. We can stress some or others, depending on what we want to do. So a form of description may be understood as a looser and less comprehensive notion than a conceptual scheme, so far as that notion has any intelligible sense. More importantly, we are thinking of whatever it is that makes formal systems not interpretable—that, too, can be a formal matter—but plausible at all.

An initial impression may be that the notion of a property can be seen as far more general, if not more basic, than that of an ingredient. It seems plausible to think about ingredients of things in a fairly literal, physical sense. Going beyond that can take us increasingly far from what we might take to be common sense, even if the notion of an ingredient is extended to a wider, technical concept of constitution or characterization. In a literal sense it seems reasonable, if uninteresting, to say that everything physical has ingredients, at least until we get to the level of quarks or strings. Despite this, the notion of a property appears to offer greater generality, if only because the notion of being an ingredient can, apparently, be subsumed within it so easily: ". . . has the property of being made of . . ." (or ". . . is made of . . .") looks like a property-based predicate capable of reducing talk about any ingredient into talk about a property. Then, for the purpose of logical manipulation, ". . . is made of . . . and . . . and . . ." looks as though it could be a conventional enough many-placed predicate or relation.

Certainly, there is no need to deny this. But there are two steps in an obvious rejoinder. First, just as we can treat ingredients as properties, perhaps for metaphysical reasons, so properties can be treated as ingredients for metaphysical reasons. Second, if that does not seem not plausible for any property, so, it might be claimed, is it implausible to treat any ingredient as a property. In other words, first, properties might be reducible to ingredients as ingredients might be reducible to properties; second, there are instances where the generality of the reduction in both directions can seem far-fetched.

In more detail, the reasons for talking about things in terms of objects with properties are hardly unfamiliar, and it would be difficult to deny that the motivation is broadly philosophical (in the sense that a search for any basic or ultimate characterization of nature has often been part of philosophy).

The rationale for thinking in terms of ingredients is far less familiar and has been assembled less explicitly, and then only in idioms which read strangely today. One example can be found in Bradley, who believed he could undermine the characterization of things in terms of their properties: "The attempt to resolve the thing into properties, each a real thing, taken somehow together with independent relations, has proved an obvious failure." Properties were blurred into "qualities" which then became interdependent with relations: "Relation presupposes quality, and quality relation. Each can be something neither together with, nor apart from, the other: and the vicious circle in which they turn is not the truth about reality." And relations were said to be ". . . a development of and from the felt totality. They inadequately express, and they still imply in the background that unity apart from which diversity is nothing. Relations are unmeaning except within and on the basis of a substantial whole, and related terms, if made absolute, are forthwith destroyed. Plurality and relatedness are but features and aspects of a unity."[5] Priority was to be given to the relation of part to whole, which Bradley understood in essentialist terms. That relation, too, was then subjected to criticism.

This can be read as a repudiation of an understanding of reality in terms of things with properties. In Bradley's terms, at least, reality was made up by its constituents. The necessary relation that mattered to him should not be understood in terms of internal relational properties between individuals (as read into his views by Moore and Russell) but as some kind of necessary constitution. Bradley might say that a property-based reading of his main insights, such as

Reality necessarily has the (relational) properties of being made up by . . .

would be misleading, whereas something like

. . . necessarily make up Reality

might be seen as less unacceptable, if not wholly satisfactory.

Whatever the shortcomings of analytical detail or precision in Bradley's arguments, the general intention was plain enough. What appeared to be separate objects with distinct properties were to be seen as elements or aspects of a single reality, essentially related within it (so far as they could be regarded as separable). The metaphysical motivation was not hard to discern. Few today are likely to be attracted by the view that any properties can be treated as ingredients (modern treatments have been more likely to question properties on nominalistic grounds[6]) but we should be aware that such a view has been held, and that it can be defended, at a high price to common sense—a price that never bothered its past supporters.

If the motivation for the treatment of properties as ingredients could only be called patently metaphysical, what can be said about an assimilation of ingredients into properties? For the sake of argument, we can assume that this reduction could be applied to all statements about ingredients, opening the way to simplified formal manipulation. But before anyone cared about formal logic, there must have been some other kind of motivation. Some writers have seen property-based description in harsh terms of overtly practical origins: "The whole notion of 'having properties' seems to me to be suspect. It may be that the notion of a thing having properties is a vestige of an animistic extension of the notion of a person having property (in the sense of chattels) to things other than persons."[7] Such speculation can at least alert us that a style of discourse is not inevitable, and to consider what its use suggests. Self-evidently, in the most general terms, discourse about objects with properties has suggested minimally that some separation between objects and properties is possible, if only conceptually. There can be an ontological suggestion that objects are what exist (as it were) solidly, leaving the status of properties to be decided afterwards. Here we stray into the well-trodden heartland of traditional metaphysics: the territory of disputes about the nature or existence of universals. Everything in this territory has been controversial, from the alleged separation of properties from objects by Plato onwards. Opponents of object-property discourse, like the author just quoted, might wish to cite the persistence of the disputes and the controversy as evidence of error in the choice of discourse. (The motivation has often been nominalistic, based on a feeling that things exist, while properties consist somehow only of what is said about them.) For now, we need only consider a thoroughgoing position that any ingredient or constituent could be describable in terms of properties. Only a philosopher could want to say that an omelet has the property of being made of eggs. Why?

It can be said that a table has properties of solidity and rectangularity. It has properties of hardness and brownness. It has properties of belonging to someone and of being situated so many millimetres from Sirius. It also has the property of being made of wood. We can try to discriminate between these various properties or to claim that some of them are not really properties of the table at all. Some philosophers have tried to show how acceptance of different kinds of property can be ontologically misleading. Berkeley or Locke, for example, would want to explore the attribution of hardness or brownness to the table. Moore or Russell might want to be critical of the thought that belonging to someone was as much a property of the table as its solidity. In the same vein one can ask what is suggested by the idea that being made of wood is a property of the table.

In one way it is harmless. In others it may be less so. An ontological trap seems to beckon if we pursue the thought that something exists such that it has the property of being made of wood. (This trap yawns still more widely with the thought that something exists that has the property of being made of one up quark and two down quarks: what is it that has this property?) Equally, a logical trap seems to beckon if we ask whether it would be the same table if it did not possess the property of being made of wood. (And, again, it looks even more painful to ask whether a neutron would be a neutron if it did not possess the property of being made of one up quark and two down quarks.)

ARISTOTLE

In Book II of his *Physics*, Aristotle launched an inquiry into what constitutes the nature (*phusis*) of a thing. He noted: "Some people think that the nature and reality of a thing which is due to nature is the primary constituent present in it, something unformed in itself. Thus in a bed it would be the wood, in a statue the bronze." He had in mind the early materialists' opinion that the nature of things is determined by their material constitution, atomic or otherwise. His case was founded on his dichotomy between matter and form. How do we define the nature of a thing? Either in terms of its matter or its form. Any account in terms of matter must be insufficient, so it has to be in terms of its form: "The form has a better claim than the matter to be called nature." He had no difficulty in satisfying himself that an account of the material making up a thing, or of the elements composing it, will be insufficient as a full account: "That which is flesh and bone only in possibility, before it acquires the form which accords with the account by which we define what flesh and bone is, does not yet have its proper nature."[8] As David Furley says, "The *nature* of a thing is not to be found in the material elements that compose it, but rather in the form that determines its composition."[9]

Aristotle's case for moving on from the constituents of a thing to other types of account was transparently thin. It came to little more than a claim that a comprehensive account of a thing's nature could not be given in terms of its constitution, together with an implication that such an account should therefore be given in some other way. The assumption that *any* account could or should be comprehensive was never justified.

There was a much more complicated discussion in *Metaphysics Zeta* 10 and 11, where Aristotle wrestled with the undeniable fact that "when we come to the individual, Socrates is composed of ultimate individual matter, and similarly in all other cases." Using heavily technical language, he ruled confidently: ". . . to bring all things . . . to Forms and to eliminate the matter is useless labor; for some things surely are a particular form in a particular matter, or particular things in a particular state." Yet the order of priority still seemed to remain clear:

> A part may be a part either of the form (i.e. the essence), or of the compound of the form and the matter, or of the matter itself. But only the parts of the form are parts of the formula, and the formula is of the universal. . . . But when we come to the concrete thing . . . of these there is no definition, but they are known by the aid of the thought or perception.

What is less clear was how this kind of priority could be explained or justified in a non-question-begging way. We find arguments like this: ". . . the semicircle is defined by the circle; and so is the finger by the whole body, for a finger is such-and-such a part of a man. Therefore the parts which are of the nature of matter, and into which as its matter a thing is divided, are posterior. . . ."[10] These have a strong air of hopeful circularity. Aristotle may only have been trying to say that a completely determinate account of something cannot, usually, be given in terms of its elements; but he would have been unwise to deny that in any case. Or he may have been insisting, quite differently, that definitions could not be given in terms of elements, but that would be an assertion, not an argument.

It may well be that in *Metaphysics Zeta*, Aristotle was trying to reconcile description by definition of essence with knowledge or acquaintance of individual material. The language of subsequent metaphysics intrudes itself irresistibly at this point. His strategy may indeed have been "to allow our two requirements on substance—or, in fact, our ordinary references to individuals—to pull the argument in opposite directions, and then to show that either direction single-mindedly pursued leads to an intolerable result,"[11] but the opposition was still presented as one between essence or definition on the one side and material content or constitution on the other, and there remained no doubt about the preferred priority of interest between these, even if neither was deemed to be wholly dispensable.[12] *Priority of interest* sounds vague because, naturally, the precise sense of priority is the central issue. To say it could be "logical" or "metaphysical" could not be to advance very far.

In any event, this may be as close as we get in Aristotle to a preference against description in terms of ingredients. There was no direct choice in favor of an alternative description in terms of properties. Nor was there an immediate, logical step on to a subject-predicate logic. The picture was more complicated.

Near the beginning of the *Categories* there is a stress on the notion of something being 'said of' something else. That turned out to be central to the logical investigation.[13] A contrast was set up at the outset between what is said of something and what is "in" it. The parts or constituents of a thing were not included in what is said of it. Aristotle also excluded them explicitly from what is *in* it, in the *Categories*: "when we spoke of things *in a subject* we did not mean things belonging in something as *parts*."[14] His common sense, as well as his investigation (presumably later) in *Metaphysics Zeta* 10 and 11, would have shown him that the parts of something are what make it up in the most literal sense.

Combinations of what is said of things make up affirmations.[15] The starting point and the drift of Aristotle's thought was from what is said, through how that can be categorized, and on to how affirmations and denials can be constructed. The finishing point, which was also the starting point for syllogistic analysis, was in the opening of the *Prior Analytics*, echoing *De Interpretatione*, where it was noted briskly that a premise or proposition—or Aristotle's unit of logical manipulation—consists of something positive or negative said about something (itself amplifying Plato's remark that a statement must be about something).[16]

Reading the same reasoning in the opposite direction, valid inference—the transmission of truth or modal value—relates to true or false statements, that is, to statements that say something about something. A statement is about something when something is said of something else. 'Saying of' is therefore a fundamental notion. What is said of something to define it is not taken to include its ingredients or constitution, but it may include other properties and relational properties.

If Aristotle were a more systematic or less subtle thinker, it would be possible to go on from here to an orderly account of essence in terms of

necessary properties: of predicates said to belong necessarily to their subjects. This is not possible for several reasons. He was not inclined to see
necessity first in terms of the necessary truth or falsity of what is said (as is
witnessed by his markedly biological approach in *Metaphysics Delta*.[17]) Nor
was his view of essence by any means nominalistic, as an orderly caricature
might suggest; the contortions of later thinkers over real essence could find
some encouragement in his works. He also had plenty to say about how
nature had to be made up—what we might see as the a priori physics and
chemistry in *De Caelo* and other scientific writings. The possible loss in systematic consistency was more than repaid by the gain from the breadth and
penetration of inquiry.

What can be said is that Aristotle bequeathed some starting points for
thought about essence in terms of necessary properties rather than constitution. That he has been a guiding light for later essentialists is scarcely
controversial. The true points of origin of medieval and recent essentialism
in his position are less readily discernible. There were two, and they are not
separate: the distillation of a preferred form of description, as where *P* is
said of *S*, and the notion that what makes up something materially could
be seen as secondary to its nature as expressed in a definition. From these
points it is not difficult to see how to reach the view that the essence of
something will consist of the properties ascribed to it necessarily. Kripke's
question "Is it a necessary or contingent property of gold that it has the
atomic number 79?" could not have been framed with such precision by
Aristotle (and not just because of the atomic number); we cannot read
back into him a use of a *de re/de dicto* distinction (from the medieval logicians). Once it has been decided that modality has to have a clear point of
location (*res* or *dictum*), it becomes hard to recapture Aristotle's helpful
ambiguity or vagueness, as it seems from today.[18] Nevertheless, Kripke's
question was plainly an aristotelian one, and not merely because it was
expressed in the terminology of post-aristotelian scholasticism. We can
locate in it the traces of the two starting points just mentioned: the
thought that the atomic number of gold can be expressed in property-
based terms—there is something (gold) which has the property of having
the atomic number 79—and the thought that the ascription of this property (even in allegedly *de re* terms) to gold is viewed as a way of characterizing its nature: ". . . present scientific theory is such that it is part of the
nature of gold as we have it to be an element with atomic number 79. It
will therefore be necessary and not contingent that gold be an element
with atomic number 79."[19]

It is valuable to go back to Aristotle to see how problematic it can be to tidy a discussion into logical terms. But what substance can be given to a suggestion that he had a significant choice of approach? In the *Physics* and the *Metaphysics*, his inquiries were not decisive, and they can be made to fit only loosely with the first steps in his logic. That is not to say they could not be made consistent with some adjustment or re-emphasis, or that Aristotle himself was guilty of some inconsistency. It could just be that he was not trying to formulate what would now be seen as an aristotelian logical theory of essences; and so he can hardly be accused of failing to do this coherently.

PARMENIDES

How could there have been any clear alternatives to anything so unclear?

Both Aristotle and Plato (in the discussion of *aitia* in the *Phaedo*[20]) were opposed to purely physical definition or explanation. But that may not be to say very much. If you are looking for a wholly exhaustive or complete form of account of things, then you will always be able to say more than could be said in an account of physical ingredients. So if the aim is a full description, an account of physical ingredients will never be enough. But such an aim is illusory. As a sufficient or determinate description, rather than a "full" description, an account of ingredients may be fine, but ancient thinkers could hardly be expected to know that.

It was not physical atomism which offered a relevantly different approach, but Parmenides. Aristotle took a poor view of him: not as dull as Melissus, but nevertheless full of error, bad arguments from false premises.[21] The case here is not that Parmenides advocated some variant, pre-aristotelian logic. Rather, he adopted so extremely different a view on language and nature that a lack of sympathy from Aristotle should be no surprise.

In the poem of Parmenides, his goddess-narrator presented both a negative and a positive account of things to her listener, "I," a "youth." Negatively, mortals were mistaken in their trust in language. "What-is" is whole and changeless . . .

> . . . wherefore it has been named all things
> That mortals have established, trusting them to be true,
> To come-to-be and to perish, to be and not to be,
> And to shift place and to exchange bright color.

"It" is not divisible since it is "all alike." When mortals talk, their use of individuations and predications will not reflect how nature is; it will not be the truth.

The goddess, on the other hand, did speak "about truth." She presented a "story" (*muthos*) about what is . . .

> . . . ungenerated and imperishable;
> Whole, single-limbed, steadfast, and complete;
> Nor was [it] once, nor will [it] be, since [it] is, now, all together,
> One, continuous; for what coming-to-be of it will you seek?[22]

and so on. Many commentators have seen a paradox.[23] The goddess was able to criticize human language while using it to expound her views—surely as foolish as a philosophical theory that all philosophy must be nonsense? In some sense it could be that true discourse is not possible for us because (in some sense) mostly we are wrong about how things are; but what about the goddess? Some writers think that what she said must be acceptable just because she was a goddess,[24] but that is hardly an excuse; if language does not work for us, why should it work for anyone? More tellingly, as Plato saw later, a name is a tool for the separation of things, as a shuttle separates a web. Without some classification of reality, discourse would not be possible at all.[25]

One interpretation can be that the goddess shows us a different way of talking. To analyse the difference in logical terms would be to beg the question, although some of the point can be understood as a matter of logical form. The characteristics mentioned by the goddess were not described as properties. They were *sêmata*, signs along a route.[26]

Nevertheless, some commentators have been misled into reading the goddess's utterances in property-based, predicative terms. The problem is that if the goddess expressed herself in subject-predicate descriptions, she forgot to mention the subject. The [it]s in the text above indicate the absence of a subject typical of the main parts of the poem. There have been three principal avenues of interpretation around this point. First, we may assume that the missing subject is Reality, Being, *Dasein*, What-is, The One. The trouble then is that the goddess does exactly what she charges erring mortals with doing: carving up Reality into separate features "apart from one another" and then talking about them.[27] Melissus did this but Parmenides did not. Second, the words of the goddess have been read as subject-predicate discourse, but with a formal rather than substantive subject. For example, "the subject is quite formal, until it is filled in with the attributes (beginning with existence) that are deduced for it." This rests on considerations such as that ". . . it needs no proving that the subject of the argument can be talked and thought about, for we are talking and thinking about it." If that were right, then it might well have been what Russell called "the first example in philosophy of an argument from thought and language to the world at large," and then, as Russell added rightly, "it cannot, of course, be accepted as valid."[28] The absurdly fallacious inference from "every predicate belongs to a subject" to "there must be one subject to which all predicates belong," frequently satirized by Russell in other contexts, may or may not have been present in the works of some Hegelian admirers of Parmenides, but it was not in his own work.

A third line of interpretation could be that subject-predicate terms are out of place. The goddess was not making true statements about the properties of something. The utterance of the goddess can be read as "*a, b, c* . . . characterize what-is" and there is the strongest temptation to take that as meaning "what-is has the (characterising) properties *a, b, c* . . ." or even "there exists *x* such that *Ax, Bx, Cx*. . . ." Yet the temptation must be resisted. It is not relevant to ask whether these forms of statement can be reduced to one another. That would amount to a question-begging insistence that logic must precede metaphysics. The result, in any event, would be to force Parmenides into a logical suit that does not fit, and then to complain that he looks absurd. Anyone can see the fallacy in going from "justice and temperance characterize a good man" to "there exists a good man who has the properties of justice and temperance." The standard Russellian route away from fallacy was through "for any x, if x is good then x is just and x is temperate." That would hardly help with Parmenides, whether or not existence is allowed as an exceptional, second-order predicate. Part of what he could have been suggesting was that predicative ascriptions must slice up the world. The true or false ascription of properties to the world might suggest that what exists could be understood apart from how it exists. Then, it might seem to a critic such as Aristotle, "Nothing can exist separately except a reality; everything else is said of a reality as underlying thing."[29] It is not hard to see why Aristotle did not like that conclusion which he saw in Parmenides. Again, Melissus might have taken this path, but Parmenides did not. Or rather, there is no reason to think that he did, apart from a desire to straitjacket him into a particular logical form.

Here is a speculative reading: Parmenides wanted to achieve not an analysis of reality into its different properties but a synthesis, bringing together characteristics of what must exist. These were not separate or independent, so we get a nonvicious circle of terms:

And it is all one to me
Where I am to begin; for I shall return there again.[30]

The outcome was not a description true of reality but was, in some direct way, the truth. Reality was not a very big thing with a lot of properties, although the naive temptation to think that is much greater than we may admit. The characteristics outlined by the goddess tell us what reality is to be.

In anachronistic logical forms, we could say that Parmenides might not accept a reduction from "a, b, c . . . characterize what-is" to "what-is has the (characterizing) properties a, b, c . . . ," or that he might prefer a reduction in the other direction, although both versions miss the point entirely. He was writing in terms which would not fit well into the requirements of aristotelian logic. It is the lack of fit that is interesting, not the fact that some modern repairs may or may not be possible or desirable. This is where we find some content in thought *before logic*. Not in the dull sense that Parmenides lived before Aristotle and was not a logician. The roots of essence in Aristotle would find no soil in the approach of Parmenides. In particular, Parmenides could give no encouragement to a preferred form of description *P is said of S*. Nor could he lead anyone to think that what makes something up could be secondary to its nature as expressed in a definition. The characteristics of nature in his poem are nonsense if read as a set of properties said to be true of a single reality.

The gain from Aristotle's approach are evident. In line with his usual practicality, he wanted a way of talking and thinking about reality which enabled him to reason about things in his world. When it came to the nature of the world itself, his form of discourse came under some strain. So, too, when it came to the constitution of the elements within the world. We can say, "three quarks make up a neutron" or "a neutron is made of three quarks." Neither is more right, nor more basic. One may be more misleading.

FREGE

Frege, more than Aristotle, seems to exemplify a self-conscious connection between a form of description and a form of logic. He felt it important to rule on what was logic and what was not. What he ruled out was not counted as an alternative to logic but as nonlogic. The support for his ruling is clearly visible: logic is about the transmission of truth; truth relates to thoughts; thoughts are articulated in a specific way. If we make judgments which split into object and concept, this suggests that we can talk about objects with properties and relations, given that "I call the concepts under which an object falls its properties."[31] But what if we talk differently? Any choice, for Frege, could not be made within logic, but before the only correct form of logic. A suggestion that there was a prior logical choice—a logically prior choice—would have implied that a different development of logic might have been possible, and he could not accept that.

In so far as he was willing to contemplate alternative starting points, it was only in his absolute rejection of them in his earlier work. The establishment of his line of thinking in "On Concept and Object" was grounded in the repudiation both of aristotelian subject-predicate discourse and of a domain-calculus as a genuine type of logic. First, ". . . instead of putting a judgement together out of an individual as subject and an already previously formed concept as predicate, we do the opposite and arrive at a concept by splitting up the content of possible judgement."[32] He produced a barrage of arguments to show how the orthodox connection (by copula) of "complete" subject with "complete" predicate could not create a "complete sense, a thought." In "On Concept and Object" there is an apparent circularity: because a thought has to be complete, if it has parts they have to be incomplete. But his thinking about the creation of a complete sense was not so much circular as self-reinforcing. The reason why he only felt able to give what he called "hints" [Winke] about his uses of *complete* and *unsaturated* was not because his subject-matter was irreducibly metaphorical (as he may have believed himself in referring to "figures of speech" [bildliche Ausdrücke]). It was because his only available explanation would be reflexive: a predicate has to be incomplete because a sentence has to be complete; a sentence has to be complete because a predicate is not. He saw this as a solution to the fin de siècle problem of the unity of judgments or propositions: "not all the parts of a thought can be complete; at least one must be 'unsaturated,' or predicative; otherwise they would not hold together."[33] *Otherwise* [sonst] here slides nicely over the reflexivity of the point. Idealists, at the same time, argued in the opposite direction. If a judgment did have "parts," then they could not hold together; there are judgments, so they can have no genuine parts.[34]

Frege was surprisingly prescriptive. He wrote of a thought "made up of parts that are not themselves thoughts":

> The simplest case of this kind is where one of the two parts is in need of supplementation and is completed by the other part, which is saturated. . . . The former part then corresponds to a concept, the latter to an object. . . . Where logic is concerned, it seems that every combination of parts results from completing something that is in need of supplementation; where logic is concerned, no whole can consist of saturated parts alone.[35]

Again, at the end of the "Critical Elucidation," as we have seen, he ruled that the "domain-calculus, in which the fundamental relation is that of part to whole, must be wholly separated from logic."[36] His arguments lacked his usual clarity. The priority of concepts to their extensions was a central Fregean tenet, argued in detail in the "Critical Elucidation" against Schröder, and against Dedekind in the Introduction to *Grundgesetze*. The priority of inference to class-inclusion in logic was enunciated more explicitly by the Kneales than by Frege: "If the elements of the [Boolean] algebra are supposed to be classes, there must clearly be a more basic theory about the derivation of propositions from other propositions." Any study of class inclusion is hard to get under way without some earlier assumptions about inference (and, as the Kneales remark, persistent blindness to this has been the defect of so-called mereologies derived from Leśniewski).[37]

We see Frege running together these two sorts of priority: "Only because classes are determined by the properties that individuals in them are to have . . . does it become possible to express thoughts in general by stating relations between classes. . . ." The arguments in the "Critical Elucidation" expressed his desire to put as much distance as possible between the relationship of object to concept and the relationship of class inclusion. But they did not entail a priority for his object-property logical form, as he may have hoped; and the passage went on ". . . only so do we get a logic."[38]

Frege's thinking can be made more understandable, if not more convincing, in a Kantian sense. His arguments about the possible form of logic, about logical form, and the form of judgment must surely be built around a Kantian skeleton. Just as for Kant "there arise exactly as many pure concepts of the understanding which apply to objects of intuition in general a priori, as there were logical functions of all possible judgments,"[39] so for Frege the possible form of judgments and logical form are interrelated: as with Kant, in the most general terms, how we can think is how we must think.

In discussing Aristotle it was important to distance him from "aristotelian essentialism," although important roots of that position (along with other, conflicting tendencies) were to be found in his work. More obviously, the origin of quantified modal logics, and the essentialism they suggest, cannot be ascribed to Frege, but a fundamental source for them is nevertheless in his thought. Just as in Aristotle there is to be found a preference for what is said of something—the properties ascribed to it—over its elements in an account of its nature, so in Frege is there a preference for a logical form in terms of object and predicative concept. Just as Aristotle's successors tried to codify essence in terms of essential properties, so some of Frege's successors have seen essence in terms of predicates belonging necessarily to, or ascribed necessarily to, objects. Aristotle's desire to repudiate metaphysical atomism led him to repudiate elements or ingredients as part of the nature of things. Frege's wish to reject a domain–calculus may have led him to put as much weight as he did on a prescriptive model of object and concept.

ESSENTIALISM

Very many philosophers have accepted object-predicate logics without going on to accept *de re* necessities or necessary properties. In a trivial sense, some sort of object-property ontology is a necessary (but not, of course, sufficient) condition for any kind of thinking about necessary or essential properties. If you believe that some things have necessary properties, then you must presuppose that some things have properties. Construal of essence in terms of necessary properties must presuppose that some things have properties which belong to them necessarily. Conversely, an understanding of reality which gives priority or precedence to a view of things as objects with properties, combined with a desire to make room for a notion of essence, can lead to a notion of things with essential properties. Once a contrast between object and properties is opened, an attempt can be made to close the implied gap by means of *de re* modality (no x without F); or some attraction may be seen in shifting any thought of modality to how we (as thinkers or speakers) associate various bundles of properties with each other.

Kripke's *Naming and Necessity* provides one clear example. Despite his interest in necessary constitution, Kripke spoke uniformly of essences in terms of properties. He was thinking about "*de re* modality, about an object having essential properties." Among "examples of essential properties" we find the property of coming from a particular origin or of being made up in a certain way. In asking "What's gold?" we ask questions like "Is it a necessary or a contingent property of gold that it has the atomic number 79?" These forms of expression indicate that Kripke saw essence in terms of necessary property-bearing; that implicitly if not overtly he favored the treatment of origin and constitution, (for instance) in terms of reduction to property-bearing. Among "many of the properties that are in fact true of Elizabeth" was the property of having been the child of certain parents and of being physically continuous with the person who had been that child.

The potential difficulties in these forms of expression should be evident from some of Kripke's examples "expressing theoretical identifications," such as "Light is a stream of photons" or "Heat is a motion of molecules" or "Water is H_2O."[40] Here, the proposed analysis was in terms of identities, but identities of necessary property-bearing. In these cases, the model of object with necessary properties was strained to the limit of credibility, not because of the (*de re*) point of application of modality and not because of the introduction of modality at all, but because the model of object with properties was itself forced to carry an intolerable burden.

Straining *to* the limit of credibility, not *beyond* it, because it is not wrong to suggest that consisting of "a motion of molecules" can be treated logically as a predicate. With enough ingenuity it can. The point, rather, is that this treatment precipitates ptolemaic complexities.[41] In basic, nontechnical terms: you can say that having certain parents is a property of yours, just as you can say that being made of eggs is a property of this omelet. You can then worry about whether you would be you if you lacked the property and whether you therefore possess it necessarily, just as you can worry about whether this omelet necessarily possesses the property of being made of eggs or whether it would be this omelet without it. Further worries can ensue. What kind of necessity is this? How is it to be explained? Where to draw the line in its application?

Perhaps all this is an option, but it is an avoidable one. That in itself is not too bold a claim in that many logicians have found the attraction of Kripke's essentialism entirely resistible. The point is about where a choice is made that leads towards essentialism. Once we start to think it is sensible to say that it is a property of this omelet to be made of eggs, then it seems reasonable (but not unavoidable) to ask whether that property is an essential or a contingent one. There is no mistaken step here, but there is a choice that can lead to certain consequences. The point of choice is in a form of expression which leads to (and is associated with) a logical form.

One might start with thinking that this table is made of these five bits of wood, just as it is brown, rectangular, hard, and so on. Kripke would have no difficulty in seeing ". . . is made of these five bits of wood" as a property-based predicate. Or, more generally, in seeing ". . . is made of . . ." as a relational property-based, two-place predicate.[42] Some writers have believed they could avert the ontological difficulties that tend to arise from this point by, in effect, treating a predicate like ". . . is made of . . ." as being itself complex in a significant way. Others have had intuitions that the property of having certain parts is intrinsically modal (". . . if y is part of x then the property of having y as one of its parts is essential to x").[43]

A stronger view is that any analysis of form, however simple or elaborate, which suggests a gap to be filled in ". . . is made of these five bits of wood" is potentially problematic in what we may be led on to think about essence. The thought, suggested earlier, that "x and y make up z" may be taken to be no less basic in form than "z has the property of being made of x and y" need not imply a formally independent logic of constitution, where a constitutive, part-whole relation takes the place of predication. Even in the simplest terms, one form can be seen as reducible to the other, as we have seen, if we treat either *x and y make up . . .* or *. . . make up z* as orthodox, unsaturated predicates. And, as argued at the beginning of this chapter, a parallel case can be assembled in the other direction: If we try hard enough (as Leśniewski and some of his followers seem to have done), we can aim to read predicates in a constitutive way, perhaps comprehensively.

CHOICE

The interesting point of choice, though, is not one between two styles of formalization, even at ground level. If it were, it would at most be a choice between logics, not a choice made before a logic gets developed. But this is not a matter of alternatives, for another, more significant reason. The important choices that are made are not between developed formal systems, where we can find reasons or preferences to adopt one rather than others. They are more at the stage where there is a movement of emphasis or interest from one viewpoint, or form of expression, to another. In the case of Aristotle, for example, we see a concentration of attention on what is said of things, in property-based descriptions. There was not even a fully reasoned exclusion of a different approach (rather the contrary, in that Aristotle was admirably even-handed), but there was a focussing of interest on one form of expression at the expense of others. This produced not so much a choice of view as a putting aside of other possible views. With Frege we find this more explicitly. He repudiated any idea of alternative basic logical forms. He was anxious to exclude forms of description that fell outside his view of correct logic.

It is right to talk in terms of emphasis, attention, or interest at a step before the affinities between notions are crystallized into definite relationships of implication or exclusion. Here is a table of such affinities:

A	B
ingredients	properties
make up	belong
comprise	characterize
essential	accidental
de re	*de dicto*
internal	external
is	said of

There can be marked affinities under A and B, but equally importantly, these affinities can only be frozen into clear relationships at the expense of creating well-recognized problems.

First, the affinities: the ingredients or elements of things make them up rather than belong to them. We may be inclined to think, with due reservations, that what makes up something may be essential to its continuous identity. Descriptions of what make things up can be in *de re* form. In so far as the constitutions of things may be said to be essential to them, we may believe that they are internal, in contrast to properties such as location or ownership. Properties may be said to belong or attach to things rather than make them up. In that they are attached, the force of their attachment may be said to be accidental or non-necessary, and hence external. What is *said of* things may be cast in a *de dicto* form.

But at every point the exceptions will be obvious, including nonessential ingredients, apparently essential properties, and so on.

Philosophical theories of essence can be produced when, to apply order or clarity, we try to tidy up these lists, to draw a firm line between them. Philosophical problems can be created in the same way: clear patterns may not fit.

Some extreme examples of theorizing are not hard to cite as supporting evidence. Bradley, for instance, could be read as a philosopher who placed as much stress as possible on list A at the expense of list B. The early, ideologically pure Quine could be said to have tried the opposite. Nor is it hard to find a case of obvious and unsuccessful compromise—Locke's theory of real essence—where there is a scarcely credible mixture of thinking about the essentiality of constitution and a desire to retain precedence for perceptible qualities.

More controversially, problems can be engendered where there is a desire to bring together intuitions from different directions. A feeling that what makes something up is essential to it, for example, can create difficulty when combined with a wish to describe what makes something up in terms of attributed properties. This can lead, as it does for Kripke, to allegedly essential properties.

∽

This now looks close to a methodological position taken by Wittgenstein: that philosophical problems are caused by the distillation of normal uses of words into explanatory theorizing. Such a position might imply that we can find the origin of philosophical talk about essence in a one-sided understanding of normal talk, that is, a "one-sided diet,"[44]—and that to appreciate this clearly might make our problems go away, or at least fall into perspective.

Whether or not such a position might have been adopted by Wittgenstein, it differs in significant ways from the view argued here. If we are to think or speak at all about modality—about what must or might be so—there can be no workable distinction between philosophical-technical and nonphilosophical-natural-ordinary contexts or vocabularies. *Essence, necessity*, and *accident* might be regarded as technical (if archaic) philosophical terms. This is questionable for *ingredient* or *property* and still more so for *must, belongs to* or *part of.* The place of Aristotelian thinking (and of latinized, postaristotelian vocabulary) in what we take to be our normal thought about essence is not calculable. Only a rootedly nonhistorical perspective could judge otherwise. If it is true that "an entire mythology is stored within in our language,"[45] then it must be true that even the barest description of that mythology has to be partly historical. The choices that can lead a philosopher's thinking towards objects with necessary properties cannot be put aside simply; nor is there any good reason why they should be. To describe a notion of essence, or, in Wittgensteinian terms, to describe how certain words are used, is to take it apart to some extent, and this procedure cannot be guaranteed to have no effect on future use. The effect may not be simple. On the one side, in reality it may not be feasible to eradicate "essentialist" thinking on the grounds that it is based on non-natural, philosophical thinking; on the other, some description of the roots of our thinking may make us less inclined to follow it.

The implication is not that we should unchoose choices that may have been made, or choose otherwise, or not think reflectively at all, or to subside into vagueness. We may get to thinking about essential properties because of perspectives based on seeing things in terms of objects with properties. These perspectives are based in millennia of thought and talk, partly grounded in metaphysical argument or in scientific methods or in successive versions of common sense. If this is right, to see it is to see why we are where we are, and it might give us some insight into a source of our problems—where they originate in conflicting intuitions, for example— but it will not in itself make these problems go away, or even suggest straightforward solutions.

CHAPTER 5

GETTING AROUND LANGUAGE

In the widest way, there can be no doubt that we have choices about how we talk. Different languages may or may not contain differing suppositions about important aspects of the world. Less evidently, as argued in the previous chapter, differing forms of discourse within a language, which may also reflect, embody or generate differing views about things, may be thought to exist. There are also differing forms of logic, or different logics, which may reflect, embody or define different forms of reasoning. The problem lies in extracting any useful clarity from these vague facts. What is the interesting difference between differing forms of discourse? How does a logic connect to a way of thinking or speaking?

The softest answers lie in the greatest and most simple clarity: different types of discourse are available, and they are the immediate foundations for different logics. So, in short, logics would be different ways of talking. Then, there might or might not be questions of legitimation or justification for the best or most suitable way of talking.

It is hard to say whether anyone has adopted such a position explicitly, although this would seem to be the outcome of the attitude taken towards the sciences by Lyotard or, more generally, by Levinas: "reason lives in language."[1] The shortage of comment on logic from writers who espouse forms of conceptual or linguistic relativism might or might not indicate sensitivity towards an area of great potential difficulty. Any suggestion that logic—or a logic—is *only* a form of discourse leaves unanswered questions about normativity.[2] The force—and, worse, the point—of logic is left unexplained.

There seems to be a dilemma. If logic lies nearer to language, it loses its strength. If it is part of how things are, it may cease to be logic and become something else: physics, for example. The previous chapters have touched on this noncommittally. What is absolutely or strongly impossible may be thought to be ruled out by how we think or talk, or by how the world is. Truth may be seen in true statements, or it may be seen, strangely, as The Truth, how things are. What must be so may be limited to how we talk about things, not how they must be. How genuine are such contrasts?

THE VEIL

Berkeley wrote in his notebook, "the chief thing I do or pretend to do is onely to remove the mist or veil of Words. This has occasion'd Ignorance & confusion. This has ruin'd the Scholemen & Mathematicians, Lawyers & Divines."

Heraclitus thought that human nature does not have right understanding, but divine nature does.

The goddess of Parmenides tells us the Truth: that what exists is whole, single, undivided. We say ("in our language") that things are separably nameable and describable. That is incorrect. So "our" use of language embodies error.

In the *Cratylus*, Socrates says that the gods call things by names that are naturally right.

So the idea of a correct way of speaking—saying how things really are—is hardly new.

Apparently similar is the opinion of Aquinas: just as God knows material things in an immaterial way, and composite things in a simple way, so he knows *enuntiabilia* not in an enuntiable way, as if there were in his intellect a division and composition of *enuntiabilia*, but he knows each thing by simple understanding, understanding the essence of each thing.[3] God sees and speaks correctly, as things are; we cannot. "Our" language is in the way. God sees and speaks directly.

Today some might be inclined to bundle these views together and to think them all equally mistaken. First, because any suggestion of direct seeing and speaking was a mistake. All saying and judging must be in some language, and any language must contain some perspective, some categorization of how things are. Further, even God can't get around language. If God were to communicate with humans, then the use of some human language would be required anyway. The goddess of Parmenides had to speak Greek to communicate the Truth. Then some will say that there is no God and so no nonhuman perspective. Or, if that is too dogmatic, it can be seen as equivalent to the previous point: even a God could not escape (some) language. An embroidered version of the same thinking might point out that the utterance of the goddess of Parmenides has to be expressible and hence self-contradictory.[4] Either way, no contrast exists to human saying.

There is some temptation to think that something said very simply might say what it says for itself, as it is. There is no other way in which it could be said. Rigid reference theories may be up this creek: some words have to stick (i.e., could not not-stick) directly onto objects. Or, again, one might think that "A transparent language offers . . . a self-interpreting description of the world. It is the world's own language."[5]

Another route is not to admit or see any point of difficulty. There are only sayings; there is nothing beyond saying. We don't oppose "language" to "the world" because language is an essential part of the ("our") world. Gadamer: "We are always already encompassed by the language that is our own."[6] So we never say that s? Not even God says that s. Only "s"? Or, a bit more sophisticated, we can believe that *saying that s* is the same as *saying that p*, and claim not to care (or need to know) what is said by *s* and *p*, so long as it is the same (so meaning drops out as irrelevant). This leads either to strong idealism or to a surreptitious peek behind some noumenal curtain.

We can ask: what is it that we want to say that we think we can't? This is not about the quest for a perfect language, an attempt to think or talk like God. The "perfection" looks like a kind of immunity against going wrong. The initial thought is that there is some flaw in how we say, in contrast with how God says, truly.

It is certainly true that how things seem ("to us")("in language") is part of how things are, not anything to be set against, in contrast with, how things are. To that extent the idea of a veil of language and the denial of that idea are both mistaken. But Parmenides himself got in first with that thought: the same thing is there for thinking and for being.[7] One modern version has been offered by John McDowell:

> In a particular experience in which one is not misled, what one takes in is *that things are thus and so. That things are thus and so* is the content of the experience, and it can also be the content of a judgement: it becomes the content of a judgement if the subject decides to take the experience at face value. So it is conceptual content. But *that things are thus and so* is also, if one is not misled, an aspect of the layout of the world: it is how things are.[8]

The trouble is that maybe we are "misled" some or all of the time. So maybe any worries are just a variant of scepticism? Historically no, not least because Parmenides was certainly no sceptic, and he was here before us. His view was that what exists really is very different from how we talk and think about it: there was no view that we can't find out how things are, or that "our senses deceive us." He was too shrewd to drag in anything like meaning; he wrote in terms of what-is and what-is-not, not what-can-be-said and what-cannot-be-said.

Some of our problems about the relation of thought (or language) and reality would not have presented themselves to Parmenides. For him, normal human language did not stand in any coherent relationship with the reality of things. As seen in chapter 4, the language of his goddess was not *about* reality. She did not offer a true account of how things are, in the sense that what she said was meant to correspond or relate to reality, as one thing said of another. To show how reality is made up may be said to be The Truth, but it was not true *of* anything.[9]

Yet even if that reading is acceptable, we might still want to insist that any identification of thought (or language) with what exists can make no useful sense. Any disquiet might stem from a persistent feeling that there has to be some significant contrast between thought and reality, and that Parmenides tried to obscure it.

But if it is fair to ask Parmenides why he wanted to emphasize what he believed to be common to thought and reality, it could be equally fair to ask why anyone might want to emphasize a distinction. In simple terms, we may be worried by identifying a list of features or characteristics with the features themselves. The worry has an epistemological base: we want to drive a wedge between x and the idea or concept of x (or the use of "x" in a language) because of the spectres of subjectivism (is my idea of x like your idea of x?), relativism (is our idea of x like their idea of x?) and idealism (is my idea of x like x?). The thoughts that feed this worry, in turn, have their origins in a subject-predicate, substance-property metaphysic. The connections are seen most clearly in the traditional Berkeleian caricature of Locke. My concept of x is my idea of it. My idea of x is also related to its qualities, the qualities which inhere in its substance. Substance-property problems then come hand-in-hand with the problems of a concept-object dichotomy. Any problem of thought and reality becomes a set of problems about perception, substance, qualities, and so on. But, once more, we can lose sight of the framework that created a problem and still feel that we should worry about the problem.

ON SAYING WHAT?

In nonhistorical, analytical terms,

"s" says that s

is always contingent. The words used to say anything could always be different, could always mean differently.[10] Or, in different terms, any language embodies or expresses some "theory" about how things are (folk metaphysics), but other theories will always be possible. So no saying, or form of saying, can be right. Yet also in some way

"s" says that s

is the best that we can do. Because we still want to be able to believe that

"s" is said + "s" says that s

tells us that

it is said that s.

In other words we want to believe that it can be said that s—that successful saying is possible. (This is not to argue that propositions or meanings must exist.)

Why believe that? Or rather how? At least three lines of reply seem to be available.

First, saying that s has to be not only possible. It cannot be possible that we could not say that s. Because then sense would be incommunicable. And it is communicable. So . . . : a transcendental argument. What is suggested by "could not" here? Our saying could not fail. There is no sense to thinking that it could fail. But that is not right, because there could be sense to it. If "sense" is "what can be imagined" or "what can be represented," then stories can be told about how sense might be failing. Things are "really" quantum-atomic, time is subjective, and so on. For Parmenides, things are really united. Individuation and predication will tear them apart. Such theorizings have to be plausible, not true.

Secondly, we are able to make things happen successfully, measure accurately, add up sums correctly; so the tools we use to do these things cannot be pragmatically blunt or ineffective. But this looks like a premise not a conclusion: we are able to understand each other, so. . . . And that has two difficulties: it looks as though it is going to presuppose the transcendental route (we could not not-understand), and it begs the question. The point of Parmenides, presumably, was that we may understand each other as well as we think we need, but we are somehow wrong or mistaken in what we understand.

Thirdly, we may want to rely on an argument that after all, we can convey truths. (Saying is possible because true saying is possible!) We may want to think that

s + it is said that s = it is true that s

but we may also hope to concertina this conveniently into

s = it is true that s.

This seems to be part of the thinking within McDowell's view quoted above. The assumption then will be that *that s* is clear ("transparent"). But it is not. Davidson wanted to read *it is said that s* as *it is said that: s*, which he took as *it is said that: "s."* That mislocated the alleged opacity.[11] The interest should focus on the step from

"s" is said + "s" says that s

to

it is said that s

that is, in the achievement of successful saying. We want to feel sure that we are saying what we say while not feeling sure how we say it. Or we may not feel sure what exactly we are saying while feeling sure that we are saying it and that we are sure of its truth. That paradox is at the heart of twentieth century philosophy of language: a paradox that echoes again the conclusion of "A Defence of Common Sense," where Moore was certain of the truth of some propositions, without being sure how they were to be "analyzed."[12] Now, we think we know what we mean, and we are sure we know that we *do* mean it, or even *must* mean it, without being sure *how* we mean it. We know what our words mean "sufficiently well to use them correctly in familiar contexts, but we do not fully understand them," as Dummett put it.

The usual line is that we need a theory of meaning first.[13] In fact we may need a theory *that meaning*, but not in an epistemological, transcendental, anti-sceptical sense of "what makes meaning possible?"

The point from Parmenides is that there is no direct contrast between meaningful utterance (goddess) and nonmeaningful (ignorant hordes). His goddess is in touch with the Truth; we are not. The question must really be about the nature of a true account, not of getting outside any ("human") form of language. Inside/outside seems plausible for languages, not for truth. You may seem to be able to get outside a particular language, but outside the Truth is only falsehood.

A misleading parallel: ideas or percepts get between my mind and how things really are. So I can never be sure what it is really like, though I can surmise it, or even feel sure that it is there (noumenally) while having no other knowledge about it. Language seems to get between our minds and how things are. So the veil of language replaces subjective consciousness. Again, this was the history constructed in Richard Rorty's *Philosophy and the Mirror of Nature* and in Ian Hacking's *Why Does Language Matter to Philosophy?*.

But language in itself does not contain illusions or misrepresentations. "What is meant" cannot be false like a wrong representation. The thought is that "language"—a system of individuations and distinctions—embodies in itself a theory of how things are. It may do, but not in a way that lends itself to a slide into relativistic clarity—getting outside, beyond, around, above.

We may be interested in what we say because we hope it may tell us something about how things are, for example about our "minds." It must tell us how we think, and how we think things are; but need tell us nothing about how they are ("really"). The point is surely that "what we are saying" alone can never tell us how things are. What we are saying has to be right, to tell us anything, after all, and that's a wholly different matter. This is a conclusion that truth is unambiguously prior to meaning.

How we mean could be very important if we are interested in the truth of what we say. But that could also be read as: How we mean could be very important if we are interested in the truth of what we say, as we say it.

A language is not a perspective, however much it seems like one. "Getting around language" is an incurably relativistic thought. There is a false analogy between seeing the unseeable (à la Berkeley) and "saying the unsayable," if only because there need be no prima facie assumption that anything is unsayable. Why should it be? Is there any reason other than an inference from the unseeable?

STARTING POINTS

As noted in chapter 2, Aquinas pointed out that the Apostles' Creed does not say that God is almighty, but "I believe in God almighty."[14] It looks as if this is the place to wheel in a distinction between *de dicto* and *de re*, especially since Aquinas contrasted *non est enuntiabile* with *sed res*; but in fact he gave a more down-to-earth reason: both in science and in faith we do not formulate statements unless, through them, we may have a knowledge of things [non enim formamus enuntiabilia nisi ut per ea de rebus cognitionem habeamus]. A footnote in the Blackfriars edition of the *Summa Theologiæ* says that "the mediation of propositions (concepts) does not impede but achieves" reference to "the real object";[15] but "mediation," surely, is exactly wrong. Where there is mediation there can be mediations, and hence alternatives, and hence right and wrong alternatives. Aquinas did not care about what we say or even what is said. The starting point was *ut . . . de rebus cognitionem habeamus*—so that we might have a knowledge of things.

That seems to come out (if only indirectly) in his discussion of angelic communication in *De Veritate*. Signs can be sensed, but angels do not use senses, so they do not use signs. Yet all speech takes place through signs, it is objected. Aquinas's response shows an interesting order of priority of knowledge over meaning. "The signs we use are sensible, because our knowledge, which is discursive, has its origin in sense-objects. But we commonly call anything a sign which, being known, leads to the knowledge of something else . . ."[16]

This can scarcely be dismissed a piece of precartesian, nonepistemological naivety; on the contrary, Aquinas started solidly from sense-perception and *cognitio*. The mode of expression will relate to, depend on, or follow from the means of knowing. How well sense is expressed, we can say, will depend on how well something is known (and angels, he believed, know very well).

It is the starting point that turns out to be crucial. Earlier, we focussed on the step between

> "s" is said + "s" says that s

and

> it is said that s.

Aquinas's thinking suggests that the direction of that step can make a great deal of difference, all the difference, in fact, in creating our perceived problems. To assume, from one direction, that saying is successfully achieved ("s" really does, successfully, say that s) and to start our thinking from successful saying, is to make an assumption that will lead to deadlock over truth and reference. That is because we want no catch in the move from *it is true that s* to *s*, that is, from what is true to what is so. Some philosophers, in fact, will see so little difficulty in such a move that they will even believe that it does not exist; what is true and what is so will be the same. But, as argued in chapter 2, that is not right. A premise, *it is said that s*, has been suppressed, and there is where all the trouble lies. After all, how "s" says that s, or how it is said that s, is meant to be deeply problematic—here we are into The Theory of Meaning! No one could ignore such trouble once immersed in it.

What Aquinas suggests is that we can take a different path. Suppose we start with what is so, for example from *nostra cognitio*; then how that is expressed may well be problematic, but we need to be clear about what the problem is and how seriously it needs to be taken.

The easy point to miss is that going from *s* to *it is said that s* does not land us in the same trouble as going from *it is said that s* to *s*. Starting from saying, we can indeed worry about how it is achieved. Here we get entangled in the veil of language. Saying, it seems, must always get between us and how things are. Here arises the quasi-sceptical problem of how we know that our language tells us how things are (how *we* know that *our* language tells us how things are—*how* we know that our language *tells* us how things are). "So it seems that we have, so to speak, no guarantee that our proposition is really a picture of reality."[17] A challenge, no doubt, but an avoidable one.

Starting from what is so, from what we know, we may still ask how it can be expressed; but from that direction, self-evidently, getting to what is so will hardly be a problem, because it is where we are already.

Such an asymmetry of perspectives, or starting points, is fundamental. In his discussions of realism, Dummett, for example, assumed that he had to start from what he called a "disputed class of statements," rather than a "disputed class of objects." Realism, as he saw it, "is a *semantic* thesis, a thesis about what, in general, renders a statement in the given class true when it is true."[18] We have to begin from what is true, that is, from what is said, not from what is known to be so. Starting from what is said, we have seen, leads us to ask how it may be said, and assumes that it is said ("successfully"). Dummett put himself in a position where what he called "realism" might appear in different ways in differing fields: "one may be a realist about a certain subject-matter, or, as it seems to me better to say, one may adopt a realistic interpretation of a certain class of statements, and not about some other subject-matter, or of some other class of statements."[19] From that starting point it was not surprising that he plunged into the theory of meaning, attaching enormous importance to it.

Yet a different perspective is possible. Dummett got into some difficulty by assuming that the necessary existence of God, *per se nota*,[20] had to be seen in terms of a "realist" understanding of a statement that God exists, or rather, as he put it, of the statement "God exists." His point could only be called oblique: the language we speak was our language "in the sense that it is we that have given to our words the meanings that they bear," yet

> it is nevertheless part of any realist interpretation of language that that meaning is such that we grasp what it is for a given sentence to be true independently of the means we have for knowing it to be true. Until a realist interpretation is shown to be untenable, there remains room for the possibility that a statement may not be capable of being known a priori by us, and yet have a meaning such that its truth-conditions could not but be fulfilled.

In addition, he wondered whether Aquinas might believe that the statement "God exists" is one of which "we can know that, if true, it is ontically, though not epistemically necessary, and which we can, further, know a posteriori to be true . . ."[21]

Though Dummett, in discussing Aquinas, distanced himself with care from any view that Aquinas might have held, it does seem plain that their perspectives were altogether different. Aquinas chose to start from what he knew, or believed, not from what was said, that is, from what was the case, not from what was true or said to be true. The difference between the question "Does God exist necessarily?" and the question "Is it necessarily true that God exists?" is not best seen in logical terms as merely a difference between *de re* and *de dicto* forms of expression, because

is it necessarily true that s

assumes that

it is true that s

which assumes that

it is said that s

which is to say that

s is said successfully.

Where we read "God exists" for "s," one of Aquinas's main points was that successful saying about God is at best not wholly straightforward.[22] We do well not to start with what is said and how we say it, but with what we know to be so. To ask whether God exists necessarily was not to ask about the *de re* necessity of a statement that God exists, but to ask whether God must exist.

Dummett's notion of differing applications of realism, presumably to allow for some specialized, realist reading of some theological statements, showed some air of desperation. There is a particular theological relevance, not surprisingly in view of the religious origins of much modern philosophy. We can think of important statements that may be held to be significant but not fully intelligible: "God became man." If we are thinking about theories of meaning, that is, if we choose to start from "a certain class of statements," then we may be forced to speculate that maybe God understands such statements where we do not (or not normally, on earth, without special illumination, perhaps). Maybe for some "reality must be as God apprehends it; and his knowledge of it guarantees that it is as it is, independently of how it appears to us or of whether we know it or can know it."[23] Maybe we do "grasp what it is for a given sentence to be true independently of the means we have for knowing it to be true." More likely, though, is that an approach from a direction of what is said, or of what "we" say, is entirely unproductive. We can go to a lot of impressive trouble to conclude, positively or critically, that we do not know how the meaning of a statement that God became man is to be described or analysed. More simply, we could say we do not understand fully how God became man. Any veil of language is an unnecessary shroud.

Shifting more widely away from theology, someone may not understand how a particle could be a wave. But the difficulty is not one of understanding a statement that a particle can be a wave. The route towards understanding does not lie through understanding how such statements can be meaningful, or even true, but through understanding how things are. This could explain the indifference of many practicing scientists to issues in the philosophy of science such as the status or modality of scientific laws.

HOW WE MUST THINK

A powerful temptation for a philosopher, even while seeing its difficulties, is the idea that we could not think without logic. This can be true by stipulation, as when reasonable thought is not possible without reason, although that truism is hardly helpful unless *reason* can be characterized noncircularly. There are ways of dressing it up, but they offer little improvement. What

Kant called "general logic" "contains the absolutely necessary rules of thinking, without which no use of the understanding takes place." For "there can
be no doubt at all: we cannot think, we cannot use our understanding,
except according to certain rules."

In unkind terms, unless you were thinking like Kant, you were not
thinking (and thus no doubt disqualified from his moral philosophy as a
rational being as such).[24] It may be easy to mock this or to hope that some
nonpsychological, depersonalized translation might be available.[25] But the
catch in the question "how do I manage to think?" is not removed by a
nonpersonal rendering as "how is thought possible?" even where, as later
with Frege, thoughts "are not the product of thinking, but are only grasped
by thinking." One way to deal with the question "Whose thoughts?" is to
answer it, like Frege, "nobody's," eternally. For him, any gap between
thought and reality was defined away by making thought not only part of
reality but, as logical thought, part of super-reality. As he noted: "My use of
the word 'thought' is out of the ordinary."[26]

Heidegger believed that Kant had erred in setting thought against reality
(or being). One can imagine an argument that a question such as "how is
(rational) thought possible?" is diametrically misplaced. Instead, we should start
from our existence as thinkers. Even the most abstractly depersonalized Kantian inquiry—what must the world be like for any (rational) judgments to be
possible?—may be thought to ignore ("forget") our presence in the world asking such a question. The assumption of a realm of my judgments separate from,
or over against, "the world," even for the purpose of discussion, might be
thought to be question-begging rather than ascetically foundationalist.[27]

In his 1935–1936 lectures published as *What Is a Thing?* Heidegger
took a more historically relativized view. Kant's approach was not so much
mistaken as a reflection of the position from which he launched it. The
question "what is a thing?" had become an historical question.[28]

⬱

It must be right that there is little point in thinking about a mistake or
a wrong answer where diverging paths may have been chosen and followed
centuries ago. The previous chapters have aimed to show how, when we
worry over truth, necessity, or limits to expression, we have already assumed
choices in directions that dictate our positions and constrain our escapes.
This is not to say that problems are illusory or disposable, but that they may
have been created by a direction of approach and a point of starting. If
things had gone differently we might have had different problems.

An extreme example is given by Wittgenstein's *Tractatus* and his later attitude to it. "Thought can never be of anything illogical, since, if it were, we should have to think illogically." The thinkable, the propositional, the sayable, the possible, and the nonillogical were identified. So "What makes logic *a priori* is the *impossibility* of illogical thought."[29] It is not hard to see how Wittgenstein got to such views, starting either from his picture-theory of saying or from his *Grundgedanke*, "that there can be no representatives of the *logic* of facts."[30] In his later work he came to say that these earlier views could be seen to stem from a determination of a use of words for a particular purpose: "what a proposition is is in one sense determined by the rules of sentence formation (in English for example), and in another sense by the use of the sign in the language-game." On the one hand, he came to realise that the basic terms in the *Tractatus* had been specified or defined to work as they did: "we call something a proposition when *in our language* we apply the calculus of truth functions to it." The "crystalline purity of logic" in the *Tractatus* was seen to be "not a *result of investigation*: it was a requirement." The propositions of logic show what thinking is.[31] On the other, he did not want to go as far as to say that logic is a linguistic creation, thus leaving unresolved questions about how far he did want to go. The balance of gains and losses was similar in structure to the balance resulting from the choice made by Leibniz, discussed in chapter 3: to deal with necessity in terms of the necessity of necessarily true propositions. There, on the one hand the gains were clear (literally, in the sense of intelligible clarity). On the other the costs were a legacy of problems about the status, force, and origin of logical truth. The path that Leibniz did not take was not without problems, either.

CHAPTER 6

"LOGIC MUST TAKE CARE OF ITSELF"

This was the opening remark in Wittgenstein's early notebooks, dated 22 August 1914, and repeated in the *Tractatus*. He called it "an extremely profound and important insight." Part of what he meant, as one commentator puts it, must have been that logic is autonomous, and "it would be the height of absurdity to speak of our making logical propositions come true." Logical validity is "independent of human choice, decision or convention. . . ." Wittgenstein wrote later that he had thought of logic as "*prior* to all experience." It "must run through all experience; no empirical cloudiness or uncertainty can be allowed to affect it—It must rather be of the purest crystal . . ."[1]

From an entirely different starting-point, Nietzsche (as already quoted) had pronounced that philosophers had erred in "mistaking the last for the first":

> They put that which comes at the end—unfortunately! for it ought
> not to come at all!—the "highest concepts," that is to say the most
> general, the emptiest concepts, the last fumes of evaporating reality, at
> the beginning, *as* the beginning. It is again only the expression of their
> way of doing reverence: the higher must not be *allowed* to grow out of
> the lower, must not be *allowed* to have grown at all . . .

He had been inveighing against the "lack of historical sense" of philosophers in a chapter called "'Reason' in Philosophy." Part of what he meant must have been that philosophical priorities had been wrong, possibly in several unseparated senses: "logically"—in that it was a mistake to imagine that the "higher" might "grow out of the lower"—but also biographically or academically. He may have doubted whether logical interests could ever have driven any philosopher's motivations.[2] It would follow that logic should not be seen in any sense as a fundamental field of study. Too much would be assumed first.

Wittgenstein wrote in his 1916 notebooks: "My work has extended from the foundations of logic to the nature of the world."[3] That could mean that he had started with logic and moved on from there to the nature of the world, or that the nature of the world was to be seen in (or through) the nature of logic. Either way, logic had been first for him, logically and (he thought) personally.

The priority of logic must be historically significant. Russell's *Critical Examination of the Philosophy of Leibniz*, from the foundational era of analytical philosophy, was quoted in chapter 3. Russell's judgment that "Leibniz's philosophy was almost entirely derived from his logic" was grounded in his identification of five premises from which the whole of Leibniz's system was meant to follow.[4] From the same period, his own theory of descriptions seemed to him (as to some others) a model of how a "logical" resolution could be offered to ancient and intractable metaphysical problems.

The Kneales note that

> It was a question much debated in antiquity whether logic should be accounted a branch of philosophy, as the Stoics said, or merely a preliminary to philosophical studies, as the Peripatetics maintained. But the dispute was little more than a quarrel about words. Both sides agreed that logic should come first in the education of a philosopher.[5]

Priority cannot be an easy subject to debate convincingly. The vague view that logic matters *a lot* in terms of priority, centrality, and consequent prestige is hard to pin down, but was surely present in the anglo-american analytical tradition, and was surely not relinquished even when Russell's version of logical foundationalism had run onto the rocks. The extremity of Wittgenstein's position, and the extremity of his reversal of it in his later thinking, may never have been shared explicitly by anyone. There have been many who have followed Frege in simply finding logic more interesting than anything else, without any theoretical justification. Later, Thomas Nagel has diagnosed what he sees as "a kind of decadence of analytic philosophy, a falling away from its origins in Frege's insistence on the fundamental importance of logic, conceived as the examination of mind-independent concepts and the development of a purer understanding and clearer expression of them."[6]

≈

Interests do not need to be justified theoretically. They can be studied historically, though this is not purely a matter of history. Priorities cannot be neutral in any sense. Presumably resting on current academic folk wisdom, an Oxford reference text asserts without argument that "moral philosophy often depends on theories of implication, which belong in logic and philosophical logic, but logic and philosophical logic do not themselves depend for their tools on moral philosophy."[7] Even this is not uncontroversial. The judgment would have been reversed for moral and philosophical reasons by Emmanuel Levinas, who regarded what he saw as the ethical as fundamental in all areas of thought. That view is remote from the perspective of analytical writers, who would be likely to dismiss it as not worth rebuttal. Yet here are some lines from Paul Celan's "Engführung":

> Der Ort, wo sie lagen, er hat
> · einen Namen—er hat
> keinen. Sie lagen nicht dort . . .[8]

Their "literal sense" could be: the place where they lie it has a name—it has none. They do not lie there. Logicians will notice two infringements of the excluded middle. Further thoughts might be that this is poetical language and (or because) its literal sense infringes the rules of standard logic. Or, more strongly, there can be no literal sense because the rules of standard logic have been broken so plainly. As Strawson put it in his *Introduction to Logical Theory*, the "*standard* purpose of speech, the intention to communicate something, is frustrated by self-contradiction."[9]

Celan's language is exceptionally factual and prosaic. Only a special crassness could insist that his lines lack sense. They include words which are, or which suggest, logical operators: *einen-keinen, nicht*. His subject can be taken to be the burial-places of his parents and all their neighbors, who disappeared in 1942, although this is not stated anywhere in his poem, or in any explanation by him.

Here the gulf of incomprehension can be wide and deep. Are we to say that Celan's aberrant or paradoxical use of language was only possible because some standard use was known or assumed? But that seems to be only a back-door reintroduction of a suggestion that the lines do lack sense.

Maybe this is a fine specimen for an intuitionist: the truth-value is unknown, so the alternatives *sie lagen* and *sie lagen nicht dort* may both remain open? Or could this be encouragement for paraconsistency?

The reality must be that Celan's lines have a surfeit, not a deficit, of meaning. It is pointless to characterise their sense as parasitically poetical. The moral shock may be amplified by the overt breach of logic. More disturbingly, part of the author's point might be that logic (even logic) has no application in a morally vacuous world. From where, he might ask, do you want to argue? The point is sharper than the trite thought that truth depends in some way on an (ultimately moral) confidence in truth-telling. The early Wittgenstein wrote that ethics must be "a condition of the world, like logic."[10]

If logic is a condition for making sense, or for expression, or for thought, then here is a serious challenge. The association explored in chapter 1, between the thinkable, the possible, and the not-illogical, is connected with a view of logic as a limiting notion; whatever else, at least contradiction is to be completely ruled out: "'Tis in vain to search for a contradiction in any thing that is distinctly conceiv'd by the mind. Did it imply any contradiction, 'tis impossible it cou'd ever be conceiv'd." Such a position does not need to be seen as wrong, but as entirely stipulative, within a particular framework. (It was to be the same, but a milder Hume who wrote a few years afterwards that "the heart of man is made to reconcile contradictions."[11]) A notion of what is absolutely ruled out, at a limit of expression or thinkability, depends on some supporting context. *Ruling out* can never be without some context of explanation and legitimation. Here was Kant, about twenty years later:

> If I now consider for a moment why that which contradicts itself
> should be absolutely nothing and impossible, I find that through the
> cancellation of the law of contradiction, the ultimate logical ground of
> all that can be thought [der letzte logische Grund alles Denklichen],
> all possibility vanishes, and there is nothing left to think.[12]

What we cannot think, "rationally" or otherwise, will always depend upon who we are, that is to say partly upon *when* we are.

As a theatre of representation, "logic" is no more impressive than human imagination. It is rather less impressive than the alleged capacities of a divine mind, as Leibniz, for one, knew well. At least the test of what God could not conceive contained some inherent and intelligible sense of legitimation.

Kant distinguished logic in a narrow, calculating sense from "reason" in his own wide sense; more on him shortly. One of the few philosophers to dispute the place of the logical as the limiting case of the rational was Ramsey, in his remarkable paper "Truth and Probability" of 1926.[13] He made unorthodox use of the orthodox distinction between deductive and inductive logic. Conventionally enough, formal deductive logic was seen as "concerned simply to ensure that our beliefs are not self-contradictory." Yet, very unconventionally, "it may well be better to be sometimes right than never right," and consistency may not always be "advantageous": "human logic or the logic of truth, which tells men how they should think, is not merely independent of but sometimes actually incompatible with formal logic." At that time Ramsey subscribed (with some reservation) to the *Tractatus* account of formal logic as tautologous, but the case he made was of wide and subversive significance. "What it may be reasonable to believe" sometimes, but not always, can be "explicable in terms of formal logic." Rules for reasonable belief may well need to refer to "the opinion of the ideal person in similar circumstances," he concluded pragmatically, in the footsteps of Peirce.[14]

It would follow that *Before Reason* (or *Before Rationality*) would be an entirely different book from *Before Logic*: the subject-matter would be unequivocally historical, sociological, or anthropological. A choice in standards of rationality need not be controversial. Nor need there be any dispute that standards in rationality have changed across history. John McDowell, for example, writes of "initiation into the space of reasons as an already going concern" as human beings are "initiated into a language." Thus "a natural language . . . serves as a repository of tradition, a store of historically accumulated wisdom about what is a reason for what."[15] But this need not be so for logic. There, choice might seem to have no place. History might seem to be only a history of discovery or development. McDowell referred to Gadamer, who had insisted that language is part of reality, that (after Heidegger) we grow up in language and live in it as we live in the rest of the world. Hence, if rationality is grounded in language, it cannot be separated from how things are, or how they have been. Equally, how things are cannot be separated from how they are understood, that is, understood through language which, conservatively for Gadamer, meant through history: "Reason exists for us only in concrete, historical terms—i.e., it is not its own master but remains constantly dependent on the given circumstances in which it operates."[16] Here he differed little in essence from Habermas, despite their other disagreements: "There is no pure reason that might don linguistic clothing only in the second place. Reason is by its very nature incarnated in contexts of communicative action and in structures of the lifeworld."[17] All this may or may not be defensible for rationality. If applied by analogy to logic it just begs the question.

THE PLACE OF CHOICE

The aim of this book has been to show how there can be choices before logic. Whether there can be choices of logics, or choices within logic, is a different matter, on which the argument should have been neutral. For those who identify logic with formal systems and their interpretations, the notion of a single, fundamental logical system excluding any other choice would be hard to defend; but that is not at issue here. There are connections between choices made before logic and particular logical positions, although that does not imply that different logics can (or cannot) be chosen.

Chapter 2, for instance, illustrates the costs and gains from the treatment of truth in terms of the truth of what is said. This is not to suggest that some different logic might be (or might have been) developed on some different footing. A location of truth in what is said (or thought or judged) may have offered great gains in logical understanding. But that depersonalized location may have abstracted truth from other contexts which endowed it with its value: moral or aesthetic truth, the truthfulness of a trusted witness or storyteller. The result may be a useful instrument, but one whose use becomes hard to characterize.

Similarly, chapter 3 shows how attitudes to the explanation of necessities are not separable from the ways in which necessities are understood. As a general claim, that is scarcely contentious. Many writers have repudiated necessity or sought to treat it reductively in terms of language-use, exactly because they have regarded it as ontologically or epistemologically inexplicable. More controversially, a view that a treatment of necessity should be part of "modal logic," downstream from propositional logic and predicate logic and still further downstream from discussions about truth, meaning, and inference, contains question-begging assumptions. In as much as the force of inference can be seen as part of the force of what must be so, any priority of treatment of what must be so will relate immediately to an understanding of logic. The degree of need for an explanation of what must be so will relate immediately to the status given to necessity.

Choice offers much scope for misunderstanding. A choice before logic sounds like a choice of how to talk, suggesting some useful contrast between how things are and how we choose to talk about them, or (more abstractly) between the content and the structure of experience. Spectres of logical relativism arise: could logic be chosen differently in different contexts of legitimation? If there are choices before logic, then must there be prelogical thought and language? And surely in the background there must be an assumption that logic is constructed by people, not discovered or revealed? So a particular theory about the nature of logic is being taken for granted after all.

These points have come up less explicitly in the course of earlier arguments, many of them in chapter 4. Someone can choose to say: this omelet has the property of being made of eggs. That form of words could then be associated with a preference towards certain logical forms, though the association is not inexorable. In fact, its looseness is the important factor. A start from such a preference may lead on to the clarification of the unclear and to the exclusion of alternatives. This is not to resort to what Ian Hacking called the myth of a "prelogical or entirely descriptive language," as if logic can be added (as a framework or structure) to some extremely simple elements (as content), before any logical choices are taken. Hacking's thought was that any bit of language must come with logical strings attached, leaving no room for anything prelogical: "Beneath any 'elementary' sentence— be it 'this is black,' said pointing at the letter 'r'—there is a swarming underworld of logically germane sentences that bear on the sentence in more than a merely empirical or inductive way."[18] Whatever there is before logic is not without logical strings, in some elemental state of pristine clarity. On the contrary, the adoption of choices may be what makes logical articulation and manipulation possible. This may seem trivial—after all, it is only a routine precaution to say what you mean (and do not mean) before starting work. There is a temptation with the subject-matter of chapter 2, for example, to protest: surely it does no harm to assume that one can disregard senses of "truth" other than the truth of true sentences, statements, or propositions, this may be a choice, but surely it is unimportant, to be left safely behind in serious studies of philosophical logic after a only prefatory glance? That might be so if the preferred truth were wholly unproblematic, clear in its sense and aims, self evident in its value. But this is hardly plausible, and in fact much of the difficulty in truth lies in what is excluded in the first selection of a clear sense to adopt.

Obviously, choices have been made by logicians. Leibniz chose to treat necessity primarily in terms of the necessary truth of propositions. Many writers have chosen to treat truth in terms of true sentences, propositions, or statements. Yet these choices are not normally seen as decisions to make some specific propositions necessary or true: that would be a gross confusion. Nor is it particularly helpful to regard such choices as linguistic, that is, as decisions about types of discourse. This can be done, of course, but that itself would be a methodological choice. A logician may seek to persuade us not to assert that 2 + 3 must = 5, but rather that the proposition (or arithmetical sentence) that 2 + 3 = 5 is necessarily true. That may be portrayed as (perhaps "nothing but") a recommendation on a choice of discourse, but only in an entirely circular way. This logician's preference is itself to treat necessity as a matter of discourse, that is, of what is said. To take the subject-matter of logic to be what is said is itself one of the most significant choices that can be made before logic. From that point there may well be problems about relations between "language" and "the world" or "reality," and about the "right" way to talk (its "logical form"), but, as argued in chapter 5, these problems may exist only from the starting point that led to them.

HOW LOGIC HAS A HISTORY

Frege believed that the phrase "the history of the development of a concept" should be avoided. "A logical concept does not develop and it does not have a history, at least not in the currently fashionable sense."[19] He would not have doubted that a history of the activities of logicians can be written. The study of logic can have a history, but logic itself may not.

Some questions in the history of logic are shared more widely by the historiography of philosophy; how far can one write about continuously existing problems of (for example) validity, inference, or modality rather than the different views of different logicians in different times? The same sort of questions can be framed about knowledge, the self, or freedom. In addition, as Frege suggested, logic presents some problems of its own. Whether validity and inference were invented, created, clarified, or discovered by Aristotle are questions with evident and extensive ramifications. Frege's implied answer was an extreme but simple one. Logic must be time-less—*there* to be discovered: "What is called the history of concepts is really a history either of our knowledge of concepts or of the meanings of words. Often it is only through enormous intellectual work, which can last for hundreds of years, that knowledge of a concept in its purity is achieved."[20] The argument of this book has been neutral on whether facts about (say) possibility were discovered by various writers, or whether concepts under a common title of possibility were invented or defined into existence.

The conclusions should be nothing like Collingwood's: "All metaphysical questions are historical questions, and all metaphysical propositions are historical propositions."[21] Where history should be important to logic is not in ontology or in legitimation, but in terms of choice and order. Choices have made a difference. Paths diverge. Going back may not be feasible.

Again, this should have emerged in the previous chapters. In chapter 1, the notion of what is absolutely impossible, or completely ruled out, was seen to have an awkward relationship with a context of representation. To be ruled out within a specified context is intelligible enough but seemingly too weak. To be ruled out in any possible context raises questions about the scope and legitimation of the governing context. The root of absolute impossibility was in some notion of what even God could not do (or think). Originally, the identification of such a notion was subversive. Before Duns Scotus, divine and human possibilities would have been seen as completely incommensurable. To bring God's capacities into any sort of contrast with nondivine possibilities—even as their idealized end point—was a dramatic step, even the first step towards a slippery slope for religion. Yet for Descartes, possibility was underwritten by the fact that our cognitive apparatus was created by God. Without the underwriting, the possibility had no force.[22] What was absolutely ruled out was ruled out by how God made us and by what even God could not do. The God of the philosophers, however implausibly, still provided a validating context for absolute impossibility, although questions about what God could do beyond human comprehension had become embarrassing. For Leibniz, a possible world was a world which God could create; and to have any explanatory value that could not be a purely circular device. Leibniz understood what some of his later imitators have missed: that no infinite field of mere alternatives could amount to possibilities. What made infinite possible worlds possible was that an infinite God could choose. The subsequent history of possibility was a series of attempts to retain the validation when the plausibility had evaporated. Hume, for example, was not at all inclined to rely on the divine creation of his mind, but was still inclined to rely on a principle that what he could represent to himself was indeed not impossible: "nothing we imagine is absolutely impossible."[23]

The central historical interest is not how possibility, or concepts of possibilities, developed. It is that the support for a use of one kind of possibility came from the plausibility of a certain context—not just from God's existence, but from the nature and activity of a specific sort of God, which seemed convincing in a specific period. And we cannot go back to that. It is historically impossible.

Such impossibility should be seen more clearly from chapter 2. Heidegger spent much of his life complaining that what might be seen as propositional truth had been a distortion of some, presumably better, preplatonic Truth. Even if his arguments were correct, his historical conclusion was a notably unhistorical one. To decide that a "wrong" intellectual turn had been taken 2,400 years ago is hardly a practical prescription for the future. (Late in his life, Heidegger himself admitted that Greek thought could be only a "point of departure."[24]) It is more valuable to grasp what may have been gained and lost in placing truth in what is said, thought, or judged. The understanding of the truth of sentences may depend on, rather than support, some wider understanding. The value of truth, why it matters, for example, may not be separated without loss from the facts about truth. None of this is to claim that a narrowed conception may have been "wrong." It has been commended for a long time and has been used productively. But in so far as truth is seen as problematic, its problems may have come from how it has been narrowed. A sociologist could have a fine time with that thought: disenchantment with an instrumentalized, depersonalized form of expression, and so on. In that speculative vein, Heidegger's approach could be judged accurately in terms of Weber's sharp diagnosis of "the need of some modern intellectuals to furnish their souls with, so to speak, genuine antiques."[25]

Chapter 3 should have brought out other ways in which history matters to logic. In a trivial sense, what counts as a problem must depend on a historical context. The interpretation of quantum mechanics worried nobody in the eighteenth century. Less obviously, what seems pressing or unimportant in logic may depend on priorities rooted in past thinking. Again in a trivial sense, the priority given to an explanation of necessity will depend on, and affect, how necessity is seen. That is most obvious at the extreme; where necessity is not accepted at all or is reduced away, no explanation will be needed, and the topic will seem uninteresting. Again, accounting for necessity may seem to be a low priority where necessity is seen as secondary or external to other topics that are more pressing. Frege is an example. Meaning and truth came first. He was able to take that position because he accepted that what must be so has to be taken as a problem about why some propositions must be true. His order of priorities in thinking about logic and his assumptions about the nature of logic were, not surprisingly, mutually supportive.

The clearest point of divergence is seen in the work of Leibniz. He had real theological worries about what must be so. He sought to resolve them by a treatment of necessarily true propositions. Subsequently, what had to be so came to look problematic, and what has to be true rather less so. The alternative he faced had been the view of Spinoza, deeply unpalatable to him for religious reasons: an association of necessity with the presence of a cause or reason, applied first to *things*, not to the truth of propositions. Spinoza's approach could have been consistent with an understanding of necessity in terms of better or worse explanation, but his own thinking was relentlessly absolutist. Once more, there could be no point in going back to some earlier thinking, as though Leibniz and his successors had just taken a wrong path. But that is far less evident for necessity than it is with truth. It is not particularly clear that any notion of necessary truth has ever been of any real benefit. It has never much impressed either mathematicians or physicists, and the schism it is supposed to have opened between them is still less impressive. "Two Dogmas of Empiricism" can be read in retrospect as suggesting that, taken in an empiricist sense, necessary truth had a lot wrong with it. To ask why some propositions absolutely must be true could have been to ask a question in a context which determined that it could have no answer.

Chapter 4 dealt with a woolly area of loose associations and plausibility. One historical thought could be summed up like this: putting on a suit of armor today does not make you a medieval knight. Essence as constitutive-properties-said-to-belong-necessarily to what they constitute may be workable with enough ingenuity; the technical apparatus may be smart. *Belonging to, made of, must* can first be latinized into *property of, constituting, necessary* and then logicised into *predicate, predicate, necessary de re* with gains and losses at both stages of translation. One gain may be that some inferential patterns will become more explicit. It could become easier to see what will follow from the information that you can make an omelet without salt, but not without eggs: no eggs, no omelet, for example. One loss can come from a failure to remember that the association between a way of talking and a form of logic is not a simple one. The routine distinction between informal and formal logic goes past the important historical point. Informal arguments can be just as valid as formal ones, but unless we know what we are talking about there can be no arguments at all. Again, this is not a matter of simple preliminary caution in the use of language. The development of some sense of essence is as much a matter of plausibility (which depends on past meanings) as of definition.

The confused origins of essence illustrate the uncertain place of clarity before logic. The point is neither that there is supposed to be unclear prelogical thought nor that clarification makes logical thought possible. At differing times there have been conflicting intuitions on the relations between constitution, property-bearing, predication, essence, and various forms of necessity. In this area it would be rash to say that there are any ahistorically correct relations to be discovered. Rather, logics or forms of logic can be developed from differing balances of interest. Clarification may be possible only at the expense of putting some intuitions to one side. A view of nature in terms of objects with properties had evident and useful metaphysical ramifications. Yet it left a notion of constitution open to implausibly reductive treatment, and left a notion of essential constitution at the fringe of credibility. A debate over whether there has been one evolving concept of essence or a series of different essences to answer different needs misses the significance of history. Frege's hopes for the eternity of concepts were beside the point. Dead concepts can be defined with the most excellent precision, but they are still dead, whether they are said to "exist" or not (*substance* is the plainest example). Again, a sociological angle is not hard to imagine.[26]

A TIME AND A PLACE

Choice and history suggest contingency. Frege's fear must have been that logic might change. If it was located in mutable human thought or language, then it would be susceptible to history.

It seems hard to avoid crude alternatives. Either logic is embodied in language or languages as an aspect of changing human culture and part of how we think and talk, or it is somehow a feature of the world we inhabit, allowing or prohibiting us to think according to rules which have nothing to do with human choice. It seems that subtler theories can be boiled down to either alternative, which in turn may appear to rest on bedrocks of ontological or religious prejudice.

Chapter 5 aimed to show how misleading these alternatives are. Some encouragement for the feeling that they *are* alternatives may have been inspired by polar contrasts between the later and earlier work of Wittgenstein. The *Tractatus* and the preceding notebooks were a classic location for the autonomy of logic. It "pervades the world" and is a "mirror-image of the world." Later, there were suggestions that it is an illusion to see the logical *must* in reality, "for we think we already see it there." Instead, the *must* of a logical proof "corresponds to a track which I lay down in language."[27] Logic appears to have shifted from reality to the rules (or "grammar") of the language used to talk about reality. In fact, for Wittgenstein, the shift may have been less decisive, mainly because of his wide sense of the "use" [Gebrauch] of language to include, typically, practical proofs and experiments. In the first part of the *Remarks on the Foundations of Mathematics*, he mulled over a view that numbers have properties, "For example, it is the property of '5' to be the subject of the rule '3 + 2 = 5'," and shifted his attention towards "processes" of proof and calculation.[28] His aim might have been to subvert a sharp dichotomy between "reality" and "language" as much as to displace logic from one to the other, but this could not be called decisive. His arguments assumed that if logic were (only) a matter of language, taken narrowly, then its force might be problematic; at least, this could be one conclusion to be drawn from all the efforts to show that proofs and experiments could be regarded as aspects of language-use.

The greatest temptation is to locate a source for the prescriptiveness or the normativity of logic in some form of transcendentalism: we could not think or talk *unless. . . .* There is an obvious hazard of circularity: rational thought is not possible without reason, and so on. More tricky to escape is the charge by Heidegger that a Kantian approach draws its strength from a subjectivist epistemology.[29] This charge becomes more, not less, pressing with a sidestep from *my* thoughts and judgments to *nobody's* impersonal thoughts, judgments, or propositions. Kant's starting point was: How can I think like this? (where, *this* includes, for example, "synthetic a priori judgments" as well as formal logic, which was to be analytic). The question was asked—it mattered—because of an alleged possibility that "I" might be wholly or importantly mistaken in my thoughts, in ways made familiar by the efforts of earlier philosophers, mainly Descartes, Hume, and Berkeley. To alter the question to "How are such thoughts or judgments possible?" is to miss the point, or rather to transfer it to a field where it loses its relevance. If thoughts or judgments are assumed to exist in a timeless realm governed by timeless laws, then how they are "possible" is hardly of interest. If thoughts are equated exhaustively with what is said or sayable ("in language") then the conditions for thought can only be linguistic conditions. Kant's starting point presented him with problems exactly because of his epistemological predicament. Logic had to be a precondition for *his* understanding of the world. If there were no constructible story about how "I" might not understand, or might understand wrongly, questions about how understanding is possible could not arise. The wider framework became more apparent in his very last writings:

God and the world are the two objects of transcendental philosophy; thinking *man* is the subject, predicate and copula. The subject who combines them in one proposition. These are logical relations in a proposition, not dealing with the existence of objects, but merely bringing what is formal in their relations of these objects to synthetic unity: God, the world, and I, man, a world-being myself, who combines the two.

Kant was explicit about his starting point: "Transcendental philosophy commences from what is subjective in reason, from the spontaneity of synthetic principles, through *ideas*. Transcendental idealism."[30]

He thought he had a way through a dilemma. In the plainest terms, if logic is to be the laws of nobody's thoughts, then what does it have to do with us? Why obey it? If it is to be the laws of "our" thought, then how can it avoid psychologism? His escape route was the transcendental hypothetical: if anyone is to think or judge, then they must think like this . . .

This is one of the most important examples of how a starting point affects not only a style of approach or a methodology but the questions that will be asked and the answers that are possible. Logic was understood by Kant in terms of content and form. The form of experience or understanding makes the content possible *for us*, or rather for any rational beings, as he might say. Without the assumptions in his account of knowledge, the contrast between form and content could have no point. Although logic was meant to draw nothing from psychology,[31] it remained an apparatus by which Kant's understanding was able to make sense of Kant's experiences as Kant thought he received them. It may be natural to hope that his choice of content might be updated and abstracted, from representations to propositions, or even to inference patterns. The strength of his approach was that, despite what he said, it was rooted in what we want to do, that is, think and act now. To purify it of content—or rather to turn its content into nobody's thoughts, meanings, or arguments—would be to take away its whole point. Logic was to be analytic—empty—but still to "constitute some of the principles necessary for ordering and systematizing knowledge elsewhere derived," as Susan Neiman puts it.[32] It was a precondition for thinking at all.

Of course, this is not to point to some logical mistake. On the contrary, Kant may have been more right that many of his successors. Once an epistemological dichotomy had been opened between the forms of experience or understanding and their content, pure thought should indeed have been empty. That, too, might have been fine when attention was focussed on forms or structures of thought or argument; but not when focussed on their normativity. Kant had in mind a direct parallel between the purity of pure general logic and pure ethics, which "contains only the necessary moral laws of a free will in general"; both were to be the rules of operation for thinkers and agents abstracted from any time or place. For him, the abstract logic of duty mirrored a duty to obey logic.[33] Far more widely, in his final writings he seems to have been trying to achieve an explicit unification of "Technical-practical and moral-practical reason and the principle which combines both in one idea." The metaphysical or epistemological background was plain enough, though the final sketch of the big picture was not:

> God and the world are ideas of moral-practical and technical-practical reason, founded on sensible representation; the former contains the predicate of personality, the latter that of. . . . Both together in one system, however, and related to each other under one principle, [are] not substances outside my thought, but rather, [they are] the thought through which we ourselves make these objects (through synthetic *a priori* cognitions from concepts) and, subjectively, are self-creators of the objects thought.

The implication might have been that the moral and the logical legitimise each other, or that they rely on a common legitimacy. (Hans Saner and subsequent commentators, including Neiman, have stressed the interdependence of moral-political-legal-religious reasoning and "pure" reasoning in Kant.[34]) Either way, there were definite presuppositions about the self and its relation to the experienced "world." Either way, Kant seemed sure enough that the self was engaged both in moral choices and in logical reflection or calculation. His direction of approach, from the subjective outwards, created and defined his problems. His direction of approach stemmed from a polarity between his mind and the world "outside" it.

≈

Once more, the aim in taking apart this history is not to imply that it should have happened differently. The conclusion should be neither that we should travel back to some point before a wrong turning was taken, nor, on the contrary, that we are trapped by decisions from the past. To see where you are and how you got there does not always leave you in the same place.

But why care about the sources of logic in past choices? If logic works, why not just get on with it? An impatience with history is understandable;

it might be an appropriate attitude for anyone who sees no philosophical problems in logic (although to see logic as a sterilized instrument must be one of the most historically-laden perspectives that could be adopted). For anyone who sees no problem in the characterization of truth or who finds necessity quite unproblematic, to take an interest in the roots of such problems might seem a waste of time. Curiosity about the roots of an indifference to these problems might seem an impertinence. Do you need reasons to be interested or not interested in anything? The illustrations in this book should have shown how some central difficulties within logic have origins in choices made outside or before logic, as do judgments about what does and does not matter.

This has a particular relevance in the history of twentieth-century philosophy. Returning to questions of priority, philosophers from Russell onwards, including later writers looking back on the thought of the century, have been inclined to see the origins of philosophy in philosophical problems which have resolved into problems of logic. That itself was an attitude with origins of some interest—some desire to transform real conflicts into questions of neutralized technique (your tools will think for you). The arguments and illustrations in this book have been intended to show how logic must be part of philosophy, not in any sense before it. Too much must come first.

NOTES

INTRODUCTION

1. M. Heidegger, *Metaphysical Foundations of Logic* (1928), tr. M. Heim (Bloomington: Indiana University Press, 1984); L. Wittgenstein, *Notebooks 1914–1916*, tr. G. E. M. Anscombe (Oxford: Blackwell, 1969), 22 August 1914 (the first entry); *Tractatus Logico-Philosophicus* (1921), tr. D. F. Pears and B. F. McGuinness (London: Routledge & Kegan Paul, 1966), 5.473.

2. *Twilight of the Idols* (1888), tr. R. J. Hollingdale (Harmondsworth: Penguin, 1990), p. 47.

3. E.g. P. F. Strawson, *The Bounds of Sense* (London: Methuen, 1966), pp. 15–24.

4. This is discussed in clear textbook terms by S. Haack, *Philosophy of Logics* (Cambridge: Cambridge University Press, 1978), pp. 1–2. There is actually a textbook, *Thinking about Logic*, subtitled *An Introduction to the Philosophy of Logic*, S. Read (Oxford: Oxford University Press, 1994).

5. Hilbert to Frege, 4 October 1895, in G. Frege, *Philosophical and Mathematical Correspondence*, eds. G. Gabriel et al., tr. H. Kaal (Oxford: Blackwell, 1980), p. 34.

6. L. Lévy-Bruhl, *Primitive Mentality* (1922), trs. L. A. Clare (London: Allen & Unwin, 1923). *Before Philosophy*, H. Frankfort et al. (Harmondsworth: Pelican, 1949) is in this tradition. A cooler discussion is in *Myth: Its Meaning and Function in Ancient and other Cultures*, G. S. Kirk (Cambridge: Cambridge University Press, 1970), pp. 238–51. Scepticism about "pre-logical mentality" is expressed by Charles Taylor, "Theories of Meaning" (1980), *Philosophical Papers* (Cambridge: Cambridge University Press, 1985), vol. I, p. 285.

7. L. E. J. Brouwer, "Consciousness, philosophy, and mathematics" (1948), in *Philosophy of mathematics: Selected readings*, eds. P. Benacerraf and H. Putnam (Cambridge: Cambridge University Press, 1983), p. 94.

8. E.g. recently, from a feminist perspective, A. Nye, *Words of Power* (London: Routledge, 1990).

9. "On the Law of Inertia" (1891), tr. H. Kaal, in *Collected Papers on Mathematics, Logic, and Philosophy*, ed. B. McGuinness (Oxford: Blackwell, 1984), p. 133.

10. A point well noted in D. H. Sanford, *If P, then Q: Conditionals and the Foundations of Reasoning* (London: Routledge, 1989), pp. 8–9.

11. W. and M. Kneale, *The Development of Logic* (Oxford: Clarendon Press, 1962), p. 511.

12. L. Wittgenstein, *Philosophical Investigations*, tr. G. E. M. Anscombe (Oxford: Blackwell, 1953) I, §124; the terminology derives from P. F. Strawson, *Individuals* (London: Methuen, 1959), Introduction.

13. "On the infinite" (1925), tr. E. Putnam and G. J. Massey, in Benacerraf and Putnam, *Philosophy of mathematics*, p. 191.

CHAPTER 1

1. To Mesland, 2 May 1644, *The Philosophical Writings of Descartes*, trs. J. Cottingham, R. Stoothoff, D. Murdoch, A. Kenny (Cambridge: Cambridge University Press, 1984 and 1991), vol. III, p. 235.

2. *De l'Ésprit géométrique* (1658), in *Oeuvres complètes*, ed. J. Chevalier (Paris: NRF/Pléiade, 1954), p. 585.

3. *Pensées*, §250, *Oeuvres*, p. 1154.

4. Descartes, Letter to Mersenne, 31 December 1640, *Philosophical Writings*, vol. III, p. 166: Il me semble bien clair qu'existentia possibilis continetur in omni eo quod clarè intelligimus, quia ex hoc ipso quod clarè intelligimus, sequitur illud à Deo posse creari.

5. *Philosophical Writings*, vol. II, p. 54.

6. S. Gaukroger, *Cartesian Logic* (Oxford: Clarendon Press, 1989), pp. 60–71.

7. *The Engines of the Soul* (Cambridge: Cambridge University Press, 1988), pp. 9–10.

8. G. Forbes, *The Metaphysics of Modality* (Oxford: Clarendon Press, 1985), p. 2. Forbes says that he is following the terminology in A. Plantinga, *The Nature of Necessity* (Oxford: Clarendon Press, 1974).

9. D. Hume, *An Abstract of a book lately published, entituled, A Treatise of Human Nature, &c* (1740), in *A Treatise of Human Nature*, ed. L. A. Selby-Bigge, revised P. H. Nidditch (Oxford: Clarendon Press, 1978), pp. 650–51.

10. 2.203, 6.362, 6.375.

11. Though, surprisingly, one not mentioned in Roy Sorensen's otherwise invaluable study, *Thought Experiments* (Oxford: Oxford University Press, 1992).

12. ". . . not the science of inference. The usefulness of deductive logic for the deductive inference of beliefs is entirely due to the realization that certain statements are jointly inconsistent," Sanford, *If P, then Q*, p. 139.

13. (1941–1942) ed. C. Lewy (London: George Allen & Unwin, 1962), p. 187.

14. Spinoza, *Theological-Political Treatise* (1670), tr. S. Shirley (Indianapolis: Hackett, 1998), I, p. 21.

15. See John Duns Scotus, *Contingency and Freedom: Lectura I, 39* (1297–1299), tr. A. Vos Jaczn. et al. (Dordrecht: Kluwer, 1994), §49ff. A claim for priority might also be made for al-Ghazâli, *The Incoherence of the Philosophers*, tr. S. A. Kamali, Lahore: Pakistan Philosophical Congress, 1958, Problem XVII, p. 194.

16. J.-L. Marion, *Sur la théologie blanche de Descartes* (Paris: Presses Universitaires de France, 1981), at the end of a discussion on this point, pp. 296–303; Descartes's "notions of necessity and possibility or rationality have no application outside the domain of truths created by God," L. Alanen and S. Knuuttila, "The Foundations of Modality and Conceivability in Descartes and his Predecessors," in ed. S. Knuuttila, *Modern Modalities: Studies of the History of Modal Theories from Medieval Nominalism to Logical Positivism* (Dordrecht: Kluwer, 1988), p. 40.

17. See p. 10 above.

18. The point is derived from Bernard Williams's reading, in *Descartes: The Project of Pure Enquiry* (Harmondsworth: Penguin, 1978), pp. 211–12.

19. F. P. Ramsey, "Truth and Probability" (1926), in *Philosophical Papers*, ed. D. H. Mellor (Cambridge: Cambridge University Press, 1990), p. 89.

20. A more formal argument for the same point was given by Ian McFetridge, "Descartes on Modality," in *Logical Necessity and other essays*, eds. J. Haldane and R. Scruton (London: Aristotelian Society, 1990), pp. 184–88.

21. I, 5.

22. *The History of Scepticism from Erasmus to Spinoza* (Berkeley: University of California Press, 1979, revised from 1960), p. 130 and note 38.

23. A. Pap, *Semantics and Necessary Truth* (New Haven: Yale University Press, 1958), p. 81.

24. Hegel, *Logic*, tr. W. Wallace (Oxford: Clarendon Press, 3rd ed., 1975, p. 204.

25. *Treatise*, I, ii, 2, p. 32.

26. *Treatise*, I, iii, 3, pp. 79–80. Arguments in this form were used many times in Book I of the *Treatise*. See D. T. Lightner, "Hume on Conceivability and Inconceivability," *Hume Studies*, XXIII, 1, April 1997, pp. 113–32. The specific application to "separability" is discussed in D. Garrett, *Cognition and Commitment in Hume's Philosophy* (Oxford: Oxford University Press, 1997), ch. 3.

27. *Letters from Ludwig Wittgenstein with a Memoir*, tr. L. Furtmüller (Oxford: Blackwell, 1967), pp. 99–100.

28. P. M. S. Hacker, on solipsism in the *Tractatus*, noted: "Unlike Kant and Schopenhauer, Wittgenstein thought that his transcendental idealist doctrines, though profoundly important, are literally inexpressible," *Insight and Illusion: Wittgenstein on Philosophy and the Metaphysics of Experience* (Oxford: Oxford University Press, 1972), p. 76.

29. Berkeley, *Alciphron*, VII, 6, in *Works*, eds. A. A. Luce and T. E. Jessop (London: Nelson, 1950), vol. 3, pp. 333–34. See Daniel E. Flage, *Berkeley's Doctrine of Notions* (London: Croom Helm, 1987), ch. 2.

30. Strictly, if its constituents had been given meanings [5.4733].

31. *Philosophical Grammar*, tr. A. Kenny, ed. R. Rhees (Oxford: Blackwell, 1974) II, §27.

32. *On Certainty*, trs. D. Paul and G. E. M. Anscombe, eds. G. E. M. Anscombe and G. H. von Wright (Oxford: Blackwell, 1969) §454; *Remarks on the Foundations of Mathematics*, tr. G. E. M. Anscombe (Oxford: Blackwell, 1967) III, §6.

33. *Philosophical Investigations*, I, §521; *Lectures on the Foundations of Mathematics, 1939*, ed. C. Diamond (University of Chicago Press, 1989), p. 146; e.g. *Remarks on the Foundations of Mathematics*, I, §79ff.

34. *Wittgenstein's Lectures, Cambridge 1932–35*, ed. A. Ambrose (Oxford: Blackwell, 1979), pp. 64–65; "Cause and Effect: Intuitive Awareness" (24 September 1937), tr. R. Rhees, in *Philosophical Occasions 1912–1951*, ed. J. Klagge and A. Nordmann (Indianapolis: Hackett, 1993), p. 373.

35. *Grammar*, II, §27; *Lectures 1932–35*, pp. 162, 63.

36. "The Question of Linguistic Idealism," in *Collected Philosophical Papers*, vol. I (Oxford: Blackwell, 1981), p. 124.

37. ". . . hängt alles an der Syntax der Wirklichkeit und Möglichkeit," *Philosophical Remarks*, trs. R. Hargreaves and R. White, ed. R. Rhees (Oxford: Blackwell, 1975), §141.

38. Colin McGinn uses this term in a different way, *The Character of Mind* (Oxford: Oxford University Press, 2nd ed. 1997), pp. 43–48.

39. §171.

40. *Lectures, 1939*, p. 146; *Investigations*, I, §253.

41. *The Principles of Linguistic Philosophy*, F. Waismann, ed. R. Harré (London: Macmillan, 1965) p. 339.

42. *Investigations*, I, §136; this reading follows G. P. Baker and P. M. S. Hacker: "There are no tolerably general principles which lay down necessary and sufficient conditions for combinations of words to make sense," *Language, Sense and Nonsense* (Oxford: Blackwell, 1984), p. 336, and "A Theory of Language?," G. E. M. Anscombe, in ed. I. Block, *Perspectives on the Philosophy of Wittgenstein* (Oxford: Blackwell, 1981).

43. §1; "Es darf nicht *vorstellbar* sein, daß *diese* Substitution in *diesem* Ausdruck etwas anderes ergibt. Oder: ich muß es für nicht vostellbar erklären," *Remarks on the Foundations of Mathematics*, II, §42.

44. "gewisse sehr allgemeine Naturtatsachen," *Investigations*, II, §xii; *Zettel*, trs. G. E. M. Anscombe, eds. G. E. M. Anscombe and G. H. van Wright (Oxford: Blackwell, 1967), §350; *Lectures 1932–35*, pp. 63–64.

45. *Philosophical Remarks*, p. 177.

46. *Philosophical Grammar*, II, §27. *The Trisectors*, U. Dudley (Washington: Mathematical Association of America, 1994) provides evidence that such questions should be far from rhetorical.

47. M. O'C. Drury, in ed. R. Rhees, *Ludwig Wittgenstein, Personal Recollections* (Oxford: Blackwell, 1981), p. 118.

48. *Investigations*, I, §500.

49. "game": *Philosophical Grammar*, II, §27, quoted above. For Kant, a geometrical impossibility "rests not on the concept in itself, but on its construction in space, i.e., on the conditions of space and its determinations," *Critique of Pure Reason*, trs. Paul Guyer and Allen W. Wood (Cambridge: Cambridge University Press, 1998), A221=B268.

50. "(T)o account for the character of the distinction between proof and experiment is to be equipped to understand the distinction in character between mathematical and empirical statements—the cardinal problem of the philosophy of mathematics," C. Wright, *Wittgenstein on the Foundations of Mathematics* (London: Duckworth, 1980), p. 318.

51. M. Foucault, *The Order of Things* (1966), tr. A. Sheridan (New York: Random House, 1970). The shift from the theatre of consciousness to the theatre of language was anatomised in Ian Hacking's *Why does Language Matter to Philosophy?* (Cambridge: Cambridge University Press, 1975) and Richard Rorty's *Philosophy and the Mirror of Nature* (Princeton: Princeton University Press, 1979).

52. Following the reading in Ian Hacking, "All Kinds of Possibility," *Philosophical Review*, 84, 1975, pp. 321–37.

53. See J. D. Barrow, *Impossibility: The Limits of Science and the Science of Limits* (Oxford: Oxford University Press, 1998).

54. M. Loux, Introduction to *The Possible and the Actual* (Ithaca: Cornell University Press, 1979), pp. 32–33.

55. *The Incoherence of the Philosophers*, p. 194.

56. G. Priest, *Beyond the limits of thought* (Cambridge: Cambridge University Press, 1995); P. Grim, *The Incomplete Universe: Totality, Knowledge and Truth* (Cambridge: MIT Press, 1991); E. Levinas, *Totality and Infinity* (1961), tr. A. Lingis (Pittsburgh: Duquesne University Press, 1969).

57. *Prolegomena to any Future Metaphysics*, tr. and ed., G. Hatfield (Cambridge University Press, 1997), §57, p. 106; also *Critique of Pure Reason*, A761=B789, A767=B795.

CHAPTER 2

1. F. P. Ramsey, "The Nature of Truth," in *On Truth*, eds. N. Rescher and U. Majer (Dordrecht: Kluwer, 1991), p. 6. Similar assertions are found at the beginnings

of Russell's essay "On the Nature of Truth and Falsehood" (1906), in *Philosophical Essays* (London: Allen & Unwin, 1966), pp. 147–48), and of G. E. Moore's entry on "Truth and Falsity" in Baldwin's *Dictionary* (1899), in *Selected Writings*, ed. T. Baldwin (London: Routledge, 1993), p.20.

2. "Facts and Propositions," (1927), *Philosophical Papers*, p. 38.

3. *Being and Time*, §44, tr. J. Stambaugh (Albany: SUNY Press, 1996), pp. 207–8.

4. Ramsey, "Truth and Probability" (1926), in *Philosophical Papers*, p. 87.

5. "Logic" (1897), in *Posthumous Writings*, trs. P. Long and R. White, eds. H. Hermes, F. Kambartel, F. Kaulbach (Oxford: Blackwell, 1979), p. 126.

6. In detail, in Heidegger's lectures, *Plato's Sophist* (1924–25), trs. R. Rojcewicz and A. Schuwer (Bloomington: University of Indiana Press, 1997), §§79–80; also *Metaphysical Foundations of Logic*, §9(a), pp. 127–28; "Plato's Doctrine of Truth" (1931–1940), tr. John Sallis, in *Pathmarks*, ed. W. McNeill (Cambridge: Cambridge University Press, 1998).

7. *The Route of Parmenides* (New Haven: Yale University Press, 1970), pp. 63–65; see also T. A. Fay, *Heidegger: The Critique of Logic* (Hague: Nijhoff, 1977), pp. 53–54.

8. *Being and Time*, pp. 199–201; *Critique of Pure Reason*, A293=B350.

9. "Facts and Propositions," *Philosophical Papers*, p. 39; possibly Ramsey was following Russell, who had thought that it was "almost impossible" to "divorce assertion from truth, as Frege does," *The Principles of Mathematics* (1903), (London: Routledge, 1992), §478, p. 504.

10. "Truth" (1959), in *Truth and other Enigmas* (London: Duckworth, 1978), p. 2; *Frege: Philosophy of Language* (London: Duckworth, 2nd. ed., 1981), p. 451.

11. Iris Murdoch, *Metaphysics as a Guide to Morals* (London: Chatto and Windus, 1992), p. 215.

12. "Mr Joachim's Nature of Truth," *Mind*, 16, 1907, p. 231.

13. (London: George Allen & Unwin, 1959), p. 178. A tasteless and unjustified parallel between William James and Hitler was drawn in "The Ancestry of Fascism," *In Praise of Idleness and Other Essays* (1935) (London: Unwin, 1976), p. 79.

14. *Metaphysics as a Guide to Morals*, pp. 56, 494–97.

15. *Pursuit of Truth* (Cambridge: Harvard University Press, 1990), p. 77.

16. *The Problems of Philosophy* (London: Home University Library, 1912), p. 249.

17. *An Enquiry Concerning the Principles of Morals* (1751), ed. L. A. Selby-Bigge, revised P. H. Nidditch (Oxford: Clarendon Press, 1975), Appendix I, §235, p. 286.

18. I, 980^a.

19. *Republic*, VI, 508e–509a.

20. J. Hintikka, *The Principles of Mathematics Revisited* (Cambridge University Press, 1996), pp. 15, 26, viii, 212, 128, 122, 44, 37, 35–36, 130, 42.

21. *Timæus*, 47ab; the most pointedly scored shift is at *Phædrus*, 246a.

22. Op. cit., pp. 27–24.

23. John 18, vv. 37–38 (RSV); one commentator notes that Pilate turns "from the personal to the abstract," *St John*, J. Marsh (Harmondsworth: Penguin, 1968), p. 602.

24. John 14, v. 6.

25. E.g., "To explain what it is to understand a particular expression involves explaining what that expression means; however uncertain the converse may be, this much is clear," M. Dummett, *The Interpretation of Frege's Philosophy* (London: Duckworth, 1981), p. 77; "clear" is ambitious: one handbook of style notes that the meaning of *involve* "has been diluted to a point of extreme insipidity," *Plain Words* (London: HMSO, 1973), p. 103.

26. M. A. Arbib and M. Hesse, *The Construction of Reality* (Cambridge University Press, 1986), p. 152; J. Derrida, *Grammatology* (1967), tr. G. C. Spivak (Baltimore: Johns Hopkins University Press, 1976), p. 15.

27. *Republic*, VI, 506de.

28. *Beyond Good and Evil* (1885–1886), tr. R. J. Hollingdale (Harmondsworth: Penguin, 1973), I, §1.

29. Iris Murdoch, *The Fire and the Sun* (1977), in *Existentialists and Mystics*, ed. P. Conradi (London: Chatto & Windus, 1997), p. 412.

30. *Plato's Sophist*, pp. 174, 175 (he seemed to have no interest in the *lekta* of stoic logic, e.g., p. 348); *What is called thinking* (1954) tr. J. G. Gray (New York: Harper, 1968), p. 155.

31. 260a.

32. p. 200.

33. *Metaphysics* IX, 10, 1051^b6, literal tr. M. Furth (Indianapolis: Hackett, 1985), p. 77 (Ou gar dia to hêmas oiesthai alêthôs se leukon einai ei su leukos, alla dia to se leukon einai hêmeis hoi phantes touto alêtheuomen).

34. *Summa Theologiæ*, IIaIIæ. 1, 2; *Apologia Pro Vita Sua*, ed. M. J. Svaglic (Oxford: Oxford University Press, 1967), Note A, p. 260.

35. E.g., H. Field, *Science without Numbers* (Oxford: Blackwell, 1980) pp. viii, 4, 15.

36. C. J. F. Williams, *What is Truth?* (Cambridge University Press, 1976), pp. 1, 6.

37. M. Dummett, *Frege, Philosophy of Language*, p. 456.

38. *The Nature of Truth* (Oxford: Clarendon Press, 1906), pp. 96–97, 107–8.

39. This may be the reasoning behind Nietzsche's early sceptical conclusions in his unpublished but frequently quoted paper "On Truth and Lies in a Nonmoral Sense" (1873), as in *Philosophy and Truth*, tr. and ed. D. Breazeale (Sussex: Harvester, 1979).

40. *Leviathan* (1651), ed. C. B. Macpherson (Harmondsworth: Penguin, 1968), I, 4, p. 105.

41. 1925, in *Philosophical Papers* (London: George Allen & Unwin, 1959).

42. "17 Key Sentences on Logic," no. 12 (1906 or earlier), and "Notes for Ludwig Darmstaedter (1919), in *Posthumous Writings*, pp. 175 and 253.

43. I. Hacking, "What is Logic?" *Journal of Philosophy*, 76, no. 6, 1979, pp. 290, 291, 299, 300.

44. Dummett, *Frege, Philosophy of Language*, pp. 442–44.

45. *The Gay Science* (Part V, 1887), tr. W. Kaufmann (New York: Vintage, 1974), §344, p. 283 (the *Genealogy of Morals*, III, §24, from the same time, contains similar views); M. Clark, *Nietzsche on Truth and Philosophy* (Cambridge University Press, 1990), p. 193.

CHAPTER 3

1. Spinoza, *Short Treatise on God, Man, and His Well-Being*, in *The Collected Works of Spinoza*, ed. and tr. E. Curley (Princeton: Princeton University Press, 1985), I, vi, vol 1, p. 85.

2. "On Freedom" (1679?), in *Philosophical Papers and Letters*, ed. L. E. Loemker (Dordrecht: Reidel, 1976), p. 263.

3. W. V. Quine, "Three Grades of Modal Involvement" (1953), in *The Ways of Paradox and Other Essays* (New York: Random House, 1966), pp. 174, 156–57.

4. See the quotation on p. 36 above.

5. A similar point was argued by Ian McFetridge, "Descartes on Modality," pp. 175–78, though he was looking at differences between the explanation of the truth of necessarily true propositions and their necessity; but for him their necessity was their necessary truth.

6. See p. 44 above.

7. "Causal Relations" (1967), in *Essays on Actions and Events* (Oxford: Clarendon Press, 1982), p. 161; "Reply to P. F. Strawson," in *Essays on Davidson*, eds. B. Vermazen and M. Hintikka (Oxford: Clarendon Press, 1985), p. 224.

8. "On Freedom," *Philosophical Papers and Letters*, p. 263. Leibniz's general strategy was discussed perceptively by Heidegger, *Metaphysical Foundations of Logic*, pp. 103–7.

9. "First Truths" (c. 1680–1684), in *Philosophical Papers and Letters*, pp. 267–68.

10. *Discourse on Metaphysics* (1686) §§13, 8, in *Philosophical Papers and Letters*, pp. 310–11, 307.

11. "On the radical origination of things" (1697), *Philosophical Papers and Letters*, p. 488.

12. *The Philosophy of Logical Atomism* (1918), in *Logic and Knowledge*, ed. R. C. Marsh, (London: Routledge, 1992), p. 179.

13. "Leibniz's Theories of Contingency," *Rice University Studies*, Vol. 62, No. 4, Fall 1977, p. 17.

14. B. Russell, *A Critical Examination of the Philosophy of Leibniz* (London: George Allen and Unwin, 1900 & 1937), Preface to 1937 ed., p. v.

15. "On the radical origination of things," *Philosophical Papers and Letters*, p. 488.

16. "On the Ethics of Benedict de Spinoza" (1678), *Philosophical Papers and Letters*, p. 203. Spinoza's definition of contingency is at *Ethics* IV, Definition 3.

17. *Ethics* (1677), tr. S. Shirley (Indianapolis: Hackett, 1992), Part I, Definition 7.

18. "On Freedom," *Philosophical Papers and Letters*, p. 265.

19. *Ethics* I, 33, Scholium 1 and 29.

20. *Theological-Political Treatise*, p. 21.

21. *Theological-Political Treatise*, p. 50.

22. Letter 12 (20 April 1663), *Spinoza: The Letters*, tr. S. Shirley (Indianapolis: Hackett, 1995), p. 102. "Modes" here, in effect, are individuals.

23. *Ethics* IV, Preface. *He* could as well be translated as *it*.

24. He may have thought of logical relations as causes between ideas, rather than the reverse: "one clear and distinct perception, or several taken together, can be absolutely cause of another clear and distinct perception" (Letter 211, 1666, *Letters*, p. 211). Ideas cause each other, as at *Ethics* II, 9. Logic itself may be intelligible in terms of some mechanics of ideas. So it becomes useless as a terminal explanation.

25. See p. 58 above.

26. *Critique of Pure Reason*, B3.

27. *Principles of Philosophy*, French Preface (1647), *Philosophical Writings*, vol. I, pp. 184, 189.

28. *Theological-Political Treatise*, III, p. 45; IV, p. 56; Letter 32 (20 November 1665), *Letters*, p. 192.

29. *Ethics* II, 47, Scholium.

30. In *From a Logical Point of View*, W. V. O. Quine (Cambridge: Harvard University Press, 1953).

31. Letter 12 (20 April 1663), *Letters*, pp. 103–5.

32. *Critique of Pure Reason*, A74=B100; *Jäsche Logic* (1800), tr. J. M. Young, in *Lectures on Logic* (Cambridge: Cambridge University Press, 1992), p. 570.

33. *Begriffsschrift* (1879), I, §4, in *The Frege Reader*, ed. M. Beaney (Oxford: Blackwell, 1997) p. 55. On Lotze, see L. Haaparanta, "Frege and his German Contemporaries on Alethic Modalities," in ed. Knuuttila, *Modern Modalities*, and H. Sluga, "Frege: the Early Years," in *Philosophy in History*, eds. R. Rorty, J. B. Schneewind and Q. Skinner (Cambridge: Cambridge University Press, 1984).

34. *The Principles of Logic* (1883)(Oxford: Oxford University Press, 2nd ed., 1922), vol. I, pp. 197 and 199.

35. *The Foundations of Arithmetic* (1884), §3, in *The Frege Reader*, p. 92.

36. *Being and Time*, I, 6, §44, p. 211.

CHAPTER 4

1. See p. 4, note 6 above.

2. The titles by Heidegger, already cited, and by Dummett (London: Duckworth, 1991).

3. Decisively, in the case of modern essentialism, D. H. Mellor's "Natural Kinds" (1977), in *Matters of Metaphysics* (Cambridge: Cambridge University Press, 1991).

4. "A Critical Elucidation of some Points in E. Schröder's *Lectures on the Algebra of Logic*" (1895), in *Collected Papers*, p. 228.

5. F. H. Bradley, *Appearance and Reality* (2nd ed., 1897) (Oxford: Oxford University Press, 1969), pp. 18, 21, 125.

6. See, for example, the review article by A. Oliver, "The Metaphysics of Properties," *Mind*, 105, no. 417, 1996, pp. 1–80.

7. J. H. Woodger, "Science without Properties," *British Journal of the Philosophy of Science*, 1951, p. 194.

8. *Physics*, tr. W. Charlton (Oxford: Clarendon Press, 1970), 193^a9–11, 193^b7, 193^b1–3; see also *Metaphysics Z*, 17, 1041^b11ff.

9. D. J. Furley, *The Greek Cosmologists* (Cambridge: Cambridge University Press, 1987), vol. I, p. 179.

10. *Metaphysics*, 1035^b30, 1036^b23, 1035^b31–$^a36$, 1035^b9–11, tr. W. D. Ross, in *Revised Oxford Aristotle*, ed. J. Barnes (Oxford: Oxford University Press, 1984).

11. G. E. L. Owen, "Particular and General"(1978–1979), in *Logic, Science and Dialectic*, ed. M. C. Nussbaum (London: Duckworth, 1986), p. 287.

12. Cf. J. Lear, *Aristotle: the desire to understand* (Cambridge: Cambridge University Press, 1988), p. 286.

13. *Categories and De Interpretatione*, tr. J. L. Ackrill (Oxford: Clarendon Press, 1963), 1^a20.

14. 3ᵃ31, also 1ᵃ24.

15. *Categories*, 2ᵃ5.

16. *Prior Analytics*, 24ᵃ17; *De Interpretatione*, 17ᵃ25; *Sophist*, 262e. These views would not be shared by those who see discontinuities in Aristotle's logical works; see P. T. Geach, "History of the Corruptions of Logic" (1968), in *Logic Matters* (Oxford: Blackwell, 1972).

17. 5, 1015ᵃ20.

18. See N. P. White, "The Origins of Aristotle's Essentialism," *Review of Metaphysics*, XXVI, 1972, pp. 60–63.

19. S. A. Kripke, *Naming and Necessity* (Oxford: Blackwell, 1980), pp. 123, 125.

20. Specifically *Phaedo*, 98cd.

21. E.g. *Physics* I, 2, 185ᵃ7–11.

22. Parmenides of Elea, *Fragments*, ed. and tr. D. Gallop (Toronto: University of Toronto Press, 1984), Frs. 8, 38–41; 8, 22; 8, 51; 2, 1 and 8, 1; 8, 3–6.

23. For discussion of various readings, see the author's "Parmenides and Language," *Ancient Philosophy*, 8, 1988, pp. 149–66.

24. E.g., ed. Gallop, p. 28, "superhuman authority."

25. *Cratylus*, 388bc; *Parmenides*, 135bc.

26. Parmenides, Fr. 8, 2.

27. Fr. 8, 56, quoted above. The same objection applies to "existential" readings, where what-is exists ungeneratedly, imperishably, wholly, and so on, adverbially.

28. G. E. L. Owen, "Eleatic Questions" (1960), in *Logic, Science and Dialectic*, ed. Nussbaum, pp. 16 and 15; B. Russell, *History of Western Philosophy* (London: George Allen & Unwin, 1946), p. 67.

29. Aristotle, *Physics* I, 185ᵃ31.

30. Parmenides, Fr. 5.

31. "On Concept and Object"(1892), *Collected Papers*, p. 190.

32. "Boole's logical Calculus and the Concept-script"(1880/81); see also the later "Notes for Ludwig Darmstaedter" (1919), in *Posthumous Writings*, pp. 17, 253.

33. "On Concept and Object" (1892), *Collected Papers*, pp. 193–94.

34. Cf. Bradley, *Appearance and Reality* (published one year after "On Concept and Object"), pp. 144–45.

35. "Notes for Ludwig Darmstaedter," *Posthumous Writings*, p. 254.

36. *Collected Papers*, p. 228.

37. *The Development of Logic*, p. 426; cf. D. Lewis, *Parts of Classes* (Oxford: Blackwell, 1991), pp. 72–81, which does not mention the "Critical Elucidation."

38. "Critical Elucidation," in *Collected Papers*, p. 226.

39. *Critique of Pure Reason*, A79=B105.

40. *Naming and Necessity*, pp. 110, 115, 116, 123, 113, 116.

41. One textbook contains a chapter entitled "The Incredulous Stare: Possible Worlds," Read, *Thinking about Logic*, ch. 4.

42. *Naming and Necessity*, p. 114, n. 56. See later reservations in Preface, p. 1.

43. See remarks on Leśniewski in P. Simons, *Parts* (Oxford: Clarendon Press, 1987), p. 22; R. M. Chisholm, "Parts as Essential to their Wholes," *Review of Metaphysics*, 26, 1973, p. 582.

44. *Philosophical Investigations*, I, §593.

45. Wittgenstein, "Remarks on Frazer's *Golden Bough*," in *Philosophical Occasions*, eds. J. Klagge and A. Nordmann (Indianapolis: Hackett, 1993), p. 133.

CHAPTER 5

1. J.-F. Lyotard, *The Postmodern Condition* (1979), trs. G. Bennington and B. Massumi (Minneapolis: University of Minnesota Press, 1984); Levinas, *Totality and Infinity*, p. 208.

2. As, straightforwardly, in H. Putnam, "Why Reason Can't Be Naturalized," *Synthèse* 52, 1982, pp. 1–23.

3. Berkeley, *Philosophical Commentaries*, A §642 (1707–08); Heraclitus, Fr. 78, tr. T. M. Robinson (Toronto: University of Toronto Press, 1987); *Cratylus*, 391de; *Summa Theologiæ* Ia. 14, 14. Aquinas's distinctions stemmed from Aristotle, *De Anima* III, 6.

4. as in Priest, *Beyond the limits of thought*.

5. M. Luntley, *Reason, Truth and Self* (London: Routledge, 1995), p. 48.

6. H.-G. Gadamer, "Man and Language" (1966), in *Philosophical Hermeneutics* (Berkeley: University of California Press, 1976), p. 62.

7. to gar auto noein estin te kai einai, Fr. 3.

8. J. McDowell, *Mind and World* (Cambridge: Harvard University Press, 1994), p. 26.

9. A. H. Coxon, note on Fr. 1, 29, *The Fragments of Parmenides* (Assen:Van Gorcum, 1986), p. 168.

10. Strongly: R. Rorty, *Contingency, irony, and solidarity* (Cambridge: Cambridge University Press, 1989), ch. 1.

11. "On Saying That" (1968), *Inquiries into Truth and Interpretation* (Oxford: Clarendon Press, 1984).

12. See p. 48.

13. Dummett, *The Logical Basis of Metaphysics*, pp. 13, 338.

14. non . . . quod Deus sit omnipotens, sed Credo in Deum omnipotentem, *Summa Theologiæ* 2a2æ. 1, 2.

15. Ed. T. C. O'Brian (London: Eyre and Spottiswoode, 1974) vol. 31, p. 13, note k.

16. *Quæstiones Disputatæ de Veritate*, IX, 4, tr. R. W. Mulligan (Chicago: Regnery, 1952), vol. 1, pp. 422, 426 [in nobis signa sunt sensibilia quia nostra cognitio, quæ discursiva est, a sensibilibus oritur].

17. Wittgenstein, *Notebooks 1914–1916*, p. 67e (20 June 1915).

18. "Realism and Anti-Realism," p. 465, and "Realism," p. 230, both in *The Seas of Language* (Oxford: Clarendon Press, 1993).

19. "Common Sense and Physics," *The Seas of Language*, p. 378.

20. *Summa Theologiæ*, Ia. 2, 1.

21. *Frege, Philosophy of Language*, pp. 118–20.

22. The theme of *Summa Theologiæ*, Ia. 13.

23. Dummett, *The Logical Basis of Metaphysics*, p. 348.

24. *Jäsche Logic*, p. 527; *Groundwork of the Metaphysics of Morals* (1785), in *Practical Philosophy*, tr. M. J. Gregor (Cambridge: Cambridge University Press, 1996), pp. 62–63.

25. An ambition of Strawson, in *The Bounds of Sense*.

26. Notes on Logic (1897), *Posthumous Writings*, p. 148, from the section headed "Separating a Thought from its Trappings," p. 127. This gets a bruising *ad hominem* treatment in Andrea Nye, *Words of Power*, ch. 9, and a more positive treatment in M. Dummett, *Origins of Analytical Philosophy* (London: Duckworth, 1993), ch. 4.

27. As in Strawson, *Individuals*, or more austerely, R. Harrison, *On What There Must Be* (Oxford: Clarendon Press, 1974); *Being and Time*, Introduction, II, §6, p. 21 and I, ii, §12, p. 55.

28. Characteristically, Heidegger touched on a root of standing-*against* in Kant's object, *Gegenstand*. *What Is a Thing?* (1935–1936), trs. W. B. Barton and V. Deutsch (South Bend: Regnery/Gateway, 1967), pp. 54, 137.

29. *Tractatus*, 3.03; 5.4731. Some of the roots of the thinking are explored in H.-J. Glock, "Philosophy, Thought and Language," in *Thought and Language*, ed. J. Preston (Cambridge: Cambridge University Press, 1997).

30. *Notebooks 1914–1916* (27 July–3 October 1914), pp. 6–8; *Tractatus*, 4.0312.

31. *Philosophical Investigations*, I, §§136, 107; *Remarks on the Foundations of Mathematics*, I, §133.

CHAPTER 6

1. *Notebooks 1914–1916*, p. 2e; *Tractatus Logico-Philosophicus*, 5.473; M. Black, *A Companion to Wittgenstein's Tractatus* (Cambridge: Cambridge University Press, 1964), pp. 272, 273; *Philosophical Investigations*, I, §97.

2. *Twilight of the Idols*, pp. 47, 45 (see Introduction, pp. 2–3 above); *Beyond Good and Evil*, I, 6.

3. p. 79e, 2 August 1916.

4. *Critical Examination*, p. v; see P. Hylton, *Russell, Idealism and the Emergence of Analytical Philosophy* (Oxford: Clarendon Press, 1990), pp. 152–66.

5. *The Development of Logic*, p. 737.

6. T. Nagel, *The Last Word* (Oxford: Oxford University Press, 1997), p. 37.

7. Ed. T. Honderich, *The Oxford Companion to Philosophy* (Oxford: Oxford University Press, 1995), p. 928.

8. Paul Celan, "Engführung," from *Sprachgitter* (Frankfurt am Main: S. Fischer Verlag, 1959).

9. P. F. Strawson, *Introduction to Logical Theory* (London: Methuen, 1963), p. 3.

10. Eine Bedingung der Welt, *Notebooks 1914–16* (24 July 1916), p. 77.

11. *Treatise*, I, ii, 4, p. 43; "Of the Parties of Great Britain," *Essays Moral, Political and Literary* (1741)(Oxford: Oxford University Press, 1963), p. 70.

12. "The only possible argument in support of a demonstration of the existence of God" (1763), in *Theoretical Philosophy 1755–1770*, tr. and ed. David Walford with Ralf Meerbote (Cambridge: Cambridge University Press, 1992), p. 127.

13. *Philosophical Papers*, p. 87.

14. *Philosophical Papers*, p. 89.

15. *Mind and World*, pp. 125–26, also p. 184.

16. *Truth and Method*, trs. J. Weinsheimer and D. G. Marshall (London: Sheed and Ward, 1989 revision), p. 276.

17. J. Habermas, *The Philosophical Discourse of Modernity*, tr. F. Lawrence (Cambridge: Polity, 1987), p. 322. A note refers to Hamann.

18. "What is Logic?," pp. 314–15.

19. "On the Law of Inertia," *Collected Papers*, p. 133 (more fully above, p. 5).

20. *The Foundations of Arithmetic* (1884), Introduction, in *The Frege Reader*, p. 88.

21. R. G. Collingwood, *An Essay on Metaphysics* (Oxford: Clarendon Press, 1940), p. 49.

22. See C. Pickstock, *After Writing* (Oxford: Blackwell, 1998), pp. 125–31; H. Ishiguro, "The Status of Necessity and Impossibility in Descartes," in *Essays on Descartes' Meditations*, ed. A. O. Rorty (Berkeley: University of California Press, 1986), pp. 464–66.

23. *Treatise*, I, ii, 2, p. 32.

24. Interview in *L'Express*, October 1969, quoted in Fay, *Heidegger: The Critique of Logic*, p. 54, n. 42. In the same vein, Stephen Toulmin writes, "After 300 years we

are back close to our starting point," *Cosmopolis* (Chicago: University of Chicago Press, 1992), p. 167.

25. M. Weber, "Science as a Vocation" (1918), in *From Max Weber*, eds. H. H. Gerth and C. Wright Mills (London: Routledge, 1948), p. 154.

26. E.g., E. Gellner, *Thought and Change* (London: Weidenfeld and Nicolson, 1964), pp. 181–94.

27. "Die Logik erfüllt die Welt," *Tractatus*, 5.61; "Die Logik ist . . . ein Spiegelbild der Welt," *Tractatus*, 6.13; *Philosophical Investigations*, I, §101; *Remarks on the Foundations of Mathematics*, II, §30.

28. I, §83.

29. E.g., *Being and Time*, I, vi, §43, pp. 189–93.

30. *Opus postumum* (1801?), trs. E. Förster and M. Rosen (Cambridge: Cambridge University Press, 1993), pp. 239, 242.

31. *Critique of Pure Reason*, A54=B78.

32. S. Neiman, *The Unity of Reason* (Oxford: Oxford University Press, 1994), p. 47.

33. *Critique of Pure Reason*, A52/B76–A57/B82.

34. *Opus postumum*, pp. 219, 228. (The ". . ." was Kant's.) H. Saner, *Kant's Political Thought*, tr. H. B. Ashton (Chicago: University of Chicago Press, 1983); see also "Reason and politics in the Kantian enterprise," in O. O'Neill, *Constructions of Reason*, (Cambridge: Cambridge University Press, 1989).

BIBLIOGRAPHY

Unattributed translations are by the author. No references are given for standard classical texts.

Adams, R. M. "Leibniz's Theories of Contingency." *Rice University Studies* 62, 1977.

Alanen, L. and Knuuttila, S. "The Foundations of Modality and Conceivability in Descartes and his Predecessors." In Knuuttila, ed., *Modern Modalities*.

Anscombe, G. E. M. "The Question of Linguistic Idealism." In *Collected Philosophical Papers*, I. Oxford: Blackwell, 1981.

———. "A Theory of Language?" In *Perspectives on the Philosophy of Wittgenstein*. Ed. I. Block. Oxford: Blackwell, 1981.

Arbib, M., and M. Hesse. *The Construction of Reality*. Cambridge: Cambridge University Press, 1986.

Aristotle. *Categories and De Interpretatione*. J. L. Ackrill, tr. Oxford: Clarendon Press, 1963.

———. *Metaphysics*, VII–X. M. Furth, literal tr. Indianapolis: Hackett, 1985.

———. *Metaphysics*. W. D. Ross, tr. In *The Revised Oxford Aristotle*. J. Barnes, ed. Oxford: Oxford University Press, 1984.

———. *Physics*. W. Charlton, tr. Oxford: Clarendon Press, 1970.

Baker, G., and P. M. S. Hacker. *Language, Sense and Nonsense*. Oxford: Blackwell, 1984.

Barrow, J. D. *Impossibility: The Limits of Science and the Science of Limits*. Oxford: Oxford University Press, 1998.

Benacerraf, P., and H. Putnam, eds. *Philosophy of mathematics: Selected readings*. Cambridge: Cambridge University Press, 1983.

Berkeley, G. *Works*. A. A. Luce and T. E. Jessop, eds. London: Nelson, 1950.

Black, M. *A Companion to Wittgenstein's Tractatus*. Cambridge: Cambridge University Press, 1964.

Bradley, F. H. *Appearance and Reality* (2nd ed., 1897). Oxford: Oxford University Press, 1969.

————. *The Principles of Logic* (1883). Oxford: Oxford University Press, 1922.

Brouwer, L. E. J. "Consciousness, philosophy, and mathematics" (1948). In Benacerraf and Putnam, eds., *Philosophy of mathematics*.

Celan, P. *Sprachgitter*. Frankfurt am Main: S. Fischer, 1959.

Chisholm, R. M. "Parts as Essential to their Wholes." *Review of Metaphysics*, 26, 1973.

Clark, M. *Nietzsche on Truth and Philosophy*. Cambridge: Cambridge University Press, 1990.

Collingwood, R. G. *An Essay on Metaphysics*. Oxford: Clarendon Press, 1940.

Coxon, A. H. *The Fragments of Parmenides*. Assen: Van Gorcum, 1986.

Davidson, D. "Causal Relations" (1967). In *Essays on Actions and Events*. Oxford: Clarendon Press, 1982.

————. "On Saying That" (1968). In *Inquiries into Truth and Interpretation*. Oxford: Clarendon Press, 1984.

————. "Reply to P. F. Strawson." In *Essays on Davidson*. B. Vermazen and M. Hintikka, eds. Oxford: Clarendon Press, 1985.

Derrida, J. *Of Grammatology* (1967). G. C. Spivak, tr. Baltimore: Johns Hopkins University Press, 1976.

Descartes, R. *The Philosophical Writings of Descartes*. J. Cottingham, R. Stoothoff, D. Murdoch, A. Kenny, tr. Cambridge: Cambridge University Press, 1984/91.

Drury, M. O'C. "Conversations with Wittgenstein." In R. Rhees, ed. *Ludwig Wittgenstein, Personal Recollections*. Oxford: Blackwell, 1981.

Dudley, U. *The Trisectors*. Washington DC: Mathematical Association of America, 1994.

Dummett, M. *Frege: Philosophy of Language*. London: Duckworth, 2nd ed., 1981.

————. *The Interpretation of Frege's Philosophy*. London: Duckworth, 1981.

————. *The Logical Basis of Metaphysics*. London: Duckworth, 1991.

————. *The Origins of Analytical Philosophy*. London: Duckworth, 1993.

————. *Truth and other Enigmas*. London: Duckworth, 1978.

————. *The Seas of Language*. Oxford: Clarendon Press, 1993.

Duns Scotus, J. *Contingency and Freedom: Lectura I, 39* (1297–1299). A. Vos Jaczn et al., trs. Dordrecht: Kluwer, 1994.

Engelmann, P. *Letters from Ludwig Wittgenstein with a Memoir*. L. Furtmüller, tr. Oxford: Blackwell, 1967.

Fay, T. A. *Heidegger: The Critique of Logic*. The Hague: Nijhoff, 1977.

Field, H. *Science without Numbers*. Oxford: Blackwell, 1980.

Flage, D. E. *Berkeley's Doctrine of Notions*. London: Croom Helm, 1987.

Forbes, G. *The Metaphysics of Modality*. Oxford: Clarendon Press, 1985.

Foucault, M. *The Order of Things* (1966). A. Sheridan, tr. New York: Random House, 1970.

Frankfort, H. et al. *Before Philosophy*. Harmondsworth: Pelican, 1949.

Frege, G. *The Frege Reader*. M. Beaney, ed. Oxford: Blackwell, 1997.

———. *Collected Papers on Mathematics, Logic, and Philosophy*. B. McGuinness, ed. Oxford: Blackwell, 1984.

———. *Philosophical and Mathematical Correspondence*. G. Gabriel et al., eds. H. Kaal, tr. Oxford: Blackwell, 1980.

———. *Posthumous Writings*. P. Long and R. White, trs. H. Hermes et al., eds. Oxford: Blackwell, 1979.

Furley, D. J. *The Greek Cosmologists*. Cambridge: Cambridge University Press, vol 1, 1987.

Gadamer, H.-G. *Philosophical Hermeneutics*. Berkeley: University of California Press, 1976.

———. *Truth and Method*. J. Weisenheimer and D. G. Marshall, trs. London: Sheed and Ward, 1989 revision.

Garrett, D. *Cognition and Commitment in Hume's Philosophy*. Oxford: Oxford University Press, 1997.

Gaukroger, S. *Cartesian Logic*. Oxford: Clarendon Press, 1989.

Geach, P. T. "History of the Corruptions of Logic" (1968). In *Logic Matters*. Oxford: Blackwell, 1972.

Gellner, E. *Thought and Change*. London: Weidenfeld and Nicolson, 1964.

al-Ghazâli, *The Incoherence of the Philosophers*, S. A. Kamali, tr. Lahore: Pakistan Philosophical Congress, 1958.

Glock, H.-J. "Philosophy, Thought and Language." In *Thought and Language*. J. Preston, ed. Cambridge: Cambridge University Press, 1997.

Grim, P. *The Incomplete Universe: Totality, Knowledge and Truth*. Cambridge: MIT Press, 1991.

Haack, S. *Philosophy of Logics*. Cambridge: Cambridge University Press, 1978.

Haaparanta, L. "Frege and his German Contemporaries on Alethic Modalities," in Knuttila, ed., *Modern Modalities*.

Habermas, J. *The Philosophical Discourse of Modernity*. F. Lawrence, tr. Cambridge: Polity, 1987.

Hacker, P. M. S. *Insight and Illusion: Wittgenstein on Philosophy and the Metaphysics of Experience*. Oxford: Oxford University Press, 1972.

Hacking, I. "All Kinds of Possibility." *Philosophical Review*, 84, 1975.

———. "What is Logic?" *Journal of Philosophy*, 76, 1979.

————. *Why does Language Matter to Philosophy?* Cambridge: Cambridge University Press, 1975.

Harrison, R. *On What There Must Be*. Oxford: Clarendon Press, 1974.

Hart, W. D. *The Engines of the Soul*. Cambridge: Cambridge University Press, 1988.

Hegel, G. W. F. *Logic* (1812/30). W. Wallace, tr. Oxford: Clarendon Press, 1873 &c.

Heidegger, M. *Being and Time* (1927). J. Stambaugh, tr. Albany: SUNY Press, 1996.

————. *Kant and the Problem of Metaphysics* (1929). Bloomington: Indiana University Press, 1990.

————. *Metaphysical Foundations of Logic* (1928). M. Heim, tr. Bloomington: Indiana University Press, 1984.

————. *Pathmarks*. W. McNeill, ed. Cambridge: Cambridge University Press, 1998.

————. *Plato's Sophist* (1924–1925). R. Rojcewicz and A. Schuwer, trs. Bloomington: University of Indiana Press, 1997.

————. *What is called Thinking?* (1954). J. G. Gray, tr. New York: Harper, 1968.

————. *What Is a Thing?* (1935–1936). W. B. Barton and V. Deutsch, trs. South Bend: Regnery/Gateway, 1967.

Heraclitus. *Fragments*. T. M. Robinson, tr. Toronto: University of Toronto Press, 1987.

Hilbert, D. "On the infinite" (1925). E. Putnam and G. J. Massey, trs. In *Philosophy of mathematics*. Benacerraf and Putnam, eds.

Hintikka, J. *The Principles of Mathematics Revisited*. Cambridge: Cambridge University Press, 1996.

Hobbes, T. *Leviathan* (1651). C. B. Macpherson, ed. Harmonsworth: Penguin, 1968.

Honderich, T. *The Oxford Companion to Philosophy*. Oxford: Oxford University Press, 1995.

Hume, D. *An Enquiry concerning the Principles of Morals* (1751). L. A. Selby-Bigge and P. H. Nidditch, eds. Oxford: Oxford University Press, 1975.

————. *Essays Moral, Political and Literary* (1741). Oxford: Oxford University Press, 1963.

————. *A Treatise of Human Nature* (1739/40). L. A. Selby-Bigge and P. H. Nidditch, eds. Oxford: Oxford University Press, 1978.

Hylton, P. *Russell, Idealism and the Emergence of Analytical Philosophy*. Oxford: Clarendon Press, 1990.

Ishiguro, H. "The Status of Necessity and Impossibility in Descartes." In *Essays on Descartes' Meditations*. A. O. Rorty, ed. Berkeley: University of California Press, 1986.

Joachim, H. *The Nature of Truth*. Oxford: Clarendon Press, 1906.

Kant, I. *Critique of Pure Reason*. Paul Guyer and Allen W. Wood, trs. Cambridge: Cambridge University Press, 1998.

———. *Lectures on Logic*. J. M. Young, tr. Cambridge: Cambridge University Press, 1992.

———. "The only possible argument in support of a demonstration of the existence of God" (1763). In *Theoretical Philosophy 1755–1770*. David Walford, tr. and ed. with Ralf Meerbote. Cambridge: Cambridge University Press, 1992.

———. *Opus postumum*. E. Förster and M. Rosen, trs. Cambridge: Cambridge University Press, 1993.

———. *Practical Philosophy*. M. J. Gregor, tr. Cambridge: Cambridge University Press, 1996.

———. *Prolegomena to any Future Metaphysics* (1783). G. Hatfield, tr. Cambridge: Cambridge University Press, 1997.

Kirk, G. S. *Myth: Its Meaning and Function in Ancient and other Cultures*. Cambridge: Cambridge University Press, 1970.

Kneale, W. and M. *The Development of Logic*. Oxford: Clarendon Press, 1962.

Knuuttila, S., ed. *Modern Modalities: Studies in the History of Modal Theories from Medieval Nominalism to Logical Positivism*. Dordrecht: Kluwer, 1988.

Kripke, S. A. *Naming and Necessity*. Oxford: Blackwell, 1980.

Lear, J. *Aristotle: The Desire to Understand*. Cambridge: Cambridge University Press, 1988.

Leibniz, G. W. *Philosophical Papers and Letters*. L. E. Loemker, ed. Dordrecht: Reidel, 1976.

Levinas, E. *Totality and Infinity* (1961). A. Lingis, tr. Pittsburgh: Duquesne University Press, 1969.

Lévy-Bruhl, L. *Primitive Mentality*. L. A. Clare, tr. London: Allen & Unwin, 1923.

Lewis, D. *Parts of Classes*. Oxford: Blackwell, 1991.

Lightner, D. T. "Hume on Conceivability and Inconceivability." *Hume Studies*, XXIII, 1997.

Loux, M., ed. *The Possible and the Actual*. Ithaca: Cornell University Press, 1979.

Luntley, M. *Reason, Truth and Self*. London: Routledge, 1995.

Lyotard, J.-F. *The Postmodern Condition* (1979). G. Bennington and B. Massumi, trs. Minneapolis: University of Minnesota Press, 1984.

Marion, J.-L. *Sur la théologie blanche de Descartes*. Paris: Presses Universitaires de France, 1981.

Marsh, J. *St. John*. Harmondsworth: Penguin, 1968.

Mason, R. "Parmenides and Language." *Ancient Philosophy*, 8, 1988.

McDowell, J. *Mind and World*. Cambridge: Harvard University Press, 1994.

McFetridge, I. "Descartes on Modality." In *Logical Necessity and other essays*. J. Haldane and R. Scruton, eds. London: Aristotelian Society, 1990.

McGinn, C. *The Character of Mind* (Oxford: Oxford University Press, 2nd ed., 1997).

Mellor, D. H. "Natural Kinds" (1977). In *Matters of Metaphysics*. Cambridge: Cambridge University Press, 1991.

Moore, G. E. *Commonplace Book*. C. Lewy, ed. London: Allen & Unwin, 1962.

———. "A Defence of Common Sense" (1925). In *Philosophical Papers*. London: Allen & Unwin, 1959.

———. "Mr. Joachim's *Nature of Truth*." *Mind*, 16, 1907.

———. "Truth and Falsity" in Baldwin's *Dictionary* (1899). In *Selected Writings*. T. Baldwin, ed. London: Routledge, 1993.

Mourelatos, A. *The Route of Parmenides*. New Haven: Yale University Press, 1970.

Murdoch, I. *Metaphysics as a Guide to Morals*. London: Chatto & Windus, 1992.

———. "The Fire and the Sun" (1977). In *Existentialists and Mystics*. P. Conradi, ed. London: Chatto & Windus, 1997.

Nagel, T. *The Last Word*. Oxford: Oxford University Press, 1997.

Neiman, S. *The Unity of Reason*. Cambridge: Cambridge University Press, 1994.

Newman, J. H. *Apologia Pro Vita Sua* (1864). M. J. Svaglic, ed. Oxford: Oxford University Press, 1967.

Nietzsche, F. *Beyond Good and Evil* (1885/86). R. J. Hollingdale, tr. Harmondsworth: Penguin, 1973.

———. *The Gay Science* (Part V, 1887). W. Kaufmann, tr. New York: Vintage, 1974.

———. "On Truth and Lies in a Non-Moral Sense" (1873). In *Philosophy and Truth*. D. Breazeale, tr. and ed. Sussex: Harvester, 1979.

———. *Twilight of the Idols* (1888). R. J. Hollingdale, tr. Harmondsworth: Penguin, 1990.

Nye, A. *Words of Power*. London: Routledge, 1990.

O'Neill, O. *Constructions of Reason*. Cambridge: Cambridge University Press, 1989.

Oliver, A. "The Metaphysics of Properties," *Mind*, 105, 1996.

Owen, G. E. L. *Logic, Science and Dialectic*. M. Nussbaum, ed. London: Duckworth, 1986.

Pap, A. *Semantics and Necessary Truth*. New Haven: Yale University Press, 1958.

Parmenides of Elea. *Fragments*. D. Gallop, ed. and tr. Toronto: University of Toronto Press, 1984.

Pascal, B. *Oeuvres complètes*. J. Chevalier, ed. Paris: NRF/Pléiade, 1954.

Pickstock, C. *After Writing*. Oxford: Blackwell, 1998.

Plantinga, A. *The Nature of Necessity*. Oxford: Clarendon Press, 1974.

Popkin, R. H. *The History of Scepticism from Erasmus to Spinoza.* Berkeley: University of California Press, 1979.

Priest, G. *Beyond the limits of thought.* Cambridge: Cambridge University Press, 1995.

Putnam, H. "Why Reason Can't be Naturalized." *Synthèse*, 52, 1982.

Quine, W. V. O. *Pursuit of Truth.* Cambridge: Harvard University Press, 1990.

———. "Three Grades of Modal Involvement" (1953). In *The Ways of Paradox and Other Essays.* New York: Random House, 1966.

———. "Two Dogmas of Empiricism" (1951). In *From a Logical Point of View.* Cambridge: Harvard University Press, 1953.

Ramsey, F. P. "The Nature of Truth." In *On Truth.* N. Rescher and U. Majer, eds. Dordrecht: Kluwer, 1991.

———. *Philosophical Papers.* D. H. Mellor, ed. Cambridge: Cambridge University Press, 1990.

Read, S. *Thinking about Logic.* Oxford: Oxford University Press, 1994.

Rorty, R. *Contingency, irony, and solidarity.* Cambridge: Cambridge University Press, 1989.

———. *Philosophy and the Mirror of Nature.* Princeton: Princeton University Press, 1979.

Russell, B. *A Critical Examination of the Philosophy of Leibniz* (1900). London: Allen and Unwin, 1937.

———. "The Ancestry of Fascism." In *In Praise of Idleness and Other Essays* (1935). London: Unwin, 1976.

———. *A History of Western Philosophy.* London: Allen & Unwin, 1946.

———. *My Philosophical Development.* London: Allen & Unwin, 1959.

———. "On the Nature of Truth and Falsehood" (1906). In *Philosophical Essays.* London: Allen & Unwin, 1966.

———. "The Philosophy of Logical Atomism" (1918). In *Logic and Knowledge.* R. C. Marsh, ed. London: Routledge, 1992.

———. *The Principles of Mathematics* (1903). London: Routledge, 1992.

———. *The Problems of Philosophy.* London: Home University Library, 1912.

Saner, H. *Kant's Political Thought.* E. B. Ashton, trs. Chicago: University of Chicago Press, 1973.

Sanford, D. H. *If P, then Q: Conditionals and the Foundations of Reasoning.* London: Routledge, 1989.

Simons, P. *Parts.* Oxford: Oxford University Press, 1987.

Sluga, H. "Frege: The Early Years." In *Philosophy in History.* R. Rorty et al., eds. Cambridge: Cambridge University Press, 1984.

Sorensen, R. *Thought Experiments.* Oxford: Oxford University Press, 1992.

Spinoza, B. *Ethics.* S. Shirley, tr. Indianapolis: Hackett, 1992.

————. *The Letters.* S. Shirley, tr. Indianapolis: Hackett, 1995.

————. *Short Treatise on God, Man, and His Well-Being* (c. 1660). In *The Collected Works of Spinoza.* E. Curley, ed. and tr. Princeton: Princeton University Press, 1985.

————. *Theological-Political Treatise.* S. Shirley, tr. Indianapolis: Hackett, 1998.

Strawson, P. F. *Individuals.* London: Methuen, 1959.

————. *Introduction to Logical Theory.* London: Methuen, 1963.

————. *The Bounds of Sense.* London: Methuen, 1966.

Taylor, C. "Theories of Meaning" (1980). In *Philosophical Papers,* I. Cambridge: Cambridge University Press, 1985.

Thomas Aquinas. *Quaestiones Disputatae de Veritate.* R. W. Mulligan, tr. Chicago: Regnery, 1952.

————. *Summa Theologiae.* T. C. O'Brian, ed. London: Eyre and Spottiswoode, 1974, vol. 31.

Toulmin, S. *Cosmopolis.* Chicago: University of Chicago Press, 1992.

Waismann, F. *The Principles of Linguistic Philosophy.* R. Harré, ed. London: Macmillan, 1965.

Weber, M. "Science as a Vocation" (1918). In *From Max Weber.* H. H. Gerth and C. Wright Mills, eds. London: Routledge, 1948.

White, N. P. "The Origins of Aristotle's Essentialism." *Review of Metaphysics,* 27, 1972.

Williams, B. *Descartes: The Project of Pure Enquiry.* Harmondsworth: Penguin, 1978.

Williams, C. J. F. *What is Truth?* Cambridge: Cambridge University Press, 1976.

Wittgenstein, L. "Cause and Effect: Intuitive Awareness." In *Philosophical Occasions.* Klagge and Nordmann, eds.

————. *Lectures on the Foundations of Mathematics, 1939.* C. Diamond, ed. Chicago: University of Chicago Press, 1989.

————. *Lectures, Cambridge 1932–35.* A. Ambrose, ed. Oxford: Blackwell, 1979.

————. *Notebooks 1914–1916.* G. E. M. Anscombe, tr. Oxford: Blackwell, 1969.

————. *On Certainty.* D. Paul and G. E. M. Anscombe, trs. G. E. M. Anscombe and G. H. von Wright, eds. Oxford: Blackwell, 1969.

————. *Philosophical Grammar.* A. Kenny, tr. R. Rhees, ed. Oxford: Blackwell, 1974.

————. *Philosophical Investigations.* G. E. M. Anscombe, tr. Oxford: Blackwell, 1953 &c.

————. *Philosophical Occasions 1912–51.* J. Klagge and A. Nordmann, eds. Indianapolis: Hackett, 1993.

———. *Philosophical Remarks*. R. Hargreaves and R. White, trs. R. Rhees, ed. Oxford: Blackwell, 1975.

———. *Remarks on the Foundations of Mathematics*. G. E. M. Anscombe, tr. Oxford: Blackwell, 1967.

———. "Remarks on Frazer's *Golden Bough*." In *Philosophical Occasions*. Klagge and Nordmann, eds.

———. *Tractatus Logico-Philosophicus*. D. F. Pears and B. F. McGuinness, trs. London: Routledge, 1966.

———. *Zettel*. G. E. M. Anscombe, tr. G. E. M. Anscombe and G. H. von Wright, eds. Oxford: Blackwell, 1967.

Woodger, J. H. "Science without Properties." *British Journal of the Philosophy of Science*, 1951.

Wright, C. *Wittgenstein on the Foundations of Mathematics*. London: Duckworth, 1980.

INDEX